FOG
CITY
FUNDAMENTALS

A Proofreading Skills Book

Fourth Edition

Editors

Pam Altman
Doreen Deicke

Gary Anderson, *Artist*

English Department
San Francisco State University

San Francisco, California

Pearson
Custom
Publishing

Printed in the United States of America.

39 38 37 36 35 34 33 32 31 30

PEARSON CUSTOM PUBLISHING
75 Arlington Street, Suite 300, Boston, MA 02116
A Pearson Education Company

Preface

Fog City Fundamentals was designed so it can be used on a "needs" basis--for individualized work suited to the needs of individual students. It begins with verbs and other sentence-level issues, since many students seem to want and need to begin with work at the sentence level. But some students may best be served by working first on apostrophes, homonyms or other sections on usage which come nearer the end of the book, while others may have mastered verbs and need to focus on, for example, sentence fragments. Some students will need to do many of the exercises in the book, others fewer. The book may be used in the classroom but it is not the basis for a whole course; it is not a substitute for carefully selected and sequenced work in composition but an adjunct to that work.

The purpose of the text is not to teach writing as such but to help students develop the skills that will make them better proofreaders of their own work, to refine their knowledge of the basic conventions of written English, and to sharpen their ability to see what they have actually written. It aims to help students understand when their work needs proofreading and how to proofread effectively.

We realize that we have in all likelihood not covered every issue dear to every instructor's heart, and we have no doubt failed to discover the peculiarities in each exercise. But we have intentionally omitted more sophisticated issues of sentence construction: this is a basic-skills proofreading text only.

Preface to the New Edition

It has been ten years since Fog City Fundamentals was revised. While the structure of the book is essentially the same, some of the exercises and the instructions have been rewritten so that the task is clearer to the student. We hope the latest edition is more user-friendly and that instructors familiar with the book will be pleased by the changes. We also invite comment, preferably constructive even if critical, from students and teachers alike.

Our special thanks to Nancy McDermid, San Francisco State University's Dean of Humanities, for her help in making available to us the funds needed for producing the first edition of this book. Thanks also to Kitty Quinn-Friel, Susan Talton, and Ernie Vasquez for their patience and perseverance in typing the manuscript as it evolved. Most of all we thank all our friends and colleagues whose suggestions and contributions made this book possible, in particular Kevin Conway, Michele Driscoll, Elise Earthman, Jan Gregory, Catharine Lucas, Dan Peterson, Patricia Porter, Leslie Roberts, William Robinson, Randall Roorda, Susan Skov.

Proofreading Tips

Most students know more grammar than they realize, but because we speak much more than we write, we often have trouble remembering or applying the rules of written English. Here are some proofreading tips to help:

1)   Proofread your work more than once and wait several hours after you've printed out your essay to proofread it for the final time. The more you can detach yourself from your work the easier it is to proofread. Always proofread at least once with the hard copy instead of just looking at it on the computer screen.

2)   Read your essay out loud, reading exactly what is on the page. You'll find that you can hear errors, particularly missing or misused *-s* or *-ed* endings.

3)   If you have difficulty seeing your errors, you may be focusing too much on the meaning, what you meant to write, instead of what is actually there. To distance yourself from what you meant to write, try going through your paper backwards. Begin with the last sentence, read it out loud, then proceed to the second to last sentence, and continue until you reach the beginning.

4)   If you have a lingering proofreading problem, keep the pages from the book with you when you proofread and do an extra reading just for that error. Only vigilance on your part will make the problem go away.

5)   On a computer, use spell check but not grammar check. Human grammar is too complicated and full of vagaries for a computer to check it accurately, but spelling is not. There is no excuse for spelling errors in a college-level essay.

6)   If you have a friend proofread your essay, then you are relying on someone else to do something you should learn to do for yourself. Proofread it yourself several times first and then if you have a friend help you proofread, have that person circle the sentence with the error in it first and see if that helps you find the error. This will teach you more than just allowing someone to fix it for you.

7)   Finally, there is more to writing than getting the grammar right. Writing is an art in which you try to entertain, persuade, and educate your reader. If you work hard on making your meaning clear and illustrating your ideas specifically, you will have fewer grammar and usage problems.

Table of Contents

1. Sentence Fragments

In order to punctuate sentences correctly and avoid fragments, we need to know the difference between two kinds of word groups: **phrases** and **clauses**.

We can see the difference in the following two groups of words:

1.　　birds from the big tree

2.　　birds fly from the big tree

In the second group of words, we can identify a subject-verb unit, while in the first we cannot.

To find the subject-verb units in sentences, follow these two steps:

1.　　First find the verb by applying the time test: change the time or tense of the sentence; the word you change is the verb.

　　In number 2, we can change

　　　　Birds *fly* from the big tree.
　to:　Birds *flew* from the big tree.　　(yesterday)
　or:　Birds *will fly* from the big tree.　　(tomorrow)

　　When we change the time, we have to change *fly* to *flew* or to *will fly*, so *fly* is the verb.

2.　　To find the subject, ask "Who or what *fly*?" The answer is *birds*, so *birds* is the subject of *fly*.　　　　　　　　　(verb)

A clause is a group of words with a subject-verb unit; the 2nd group of words contains the subject-verb unit *birds fly*, so it is a clause.

A phrase is a group of words without a subject-verb unit. If we try to change the time or tense of the 1st group of words, we cannot, because it contains no word that changes to show time or tense. It has no verb, so it can't have a subject-verb unit. It is a phrase.

Exercise 1

Which of the following groups of words are phrases? Which are clauses? Following the guidelines for finding subject-verb units in sentences, label each one.

| | Example: | my cousin in Virginia | phrase |
| | | my cousin lives in Virginia | clause |

---

1. a long, unpleasant trip

2. we took a long, unpleasant trip

3. some teachers have no sense of humor at all

4. teachers with no sense of humor at all

5. the creep in my psychology class

6. a small town near Half Moon Bay

7. he lives in El Granada, a small town near Half Moon Bay

8. he forgot his wallet

9. we share our money with our friends

10. rooms full of old paper, rusty kitchen equipment, and broken furniture

11. the first day of the month

12. many cats in my neighborhood are strays

Special Kinds of Phrases:

1) ***-ing* phrases**: When you look for verbs in sentences, remember that the *-ing* form of a word cannot be a verb all by itself, so the group of words

   the sweat dripping from his forehead

is a <u>phrase</u>, not a clause. To make this phrase into a clause, we need to complete the verb by adding a form of the verb *be*:

   The sweat *was dripping* from his forehead.

We can make sure that an *-ing* word is part of a verb, by checking to see if the *-ing* word follows a form of the verb *to be* (*am, is, are, was, were, will be, has been, have been, had been, will have been*).

Examples:　Trevor *is working* in a bank.
　　　　　　Trevor *was working* in a bank last year.
　　　　　　Trevor *has been working* in a bank for three years.

2) **another kind of phrase:**　It's obvious that "happy people" is a phrase. But so is "people who are happy." A special kind of phrase follows this pattern:

   noun + *who*　　　people who are happy
   noun + *which*　　habits which annoy me
   noun + *that*　　　dog that lives next door

Even though these structures contain a verb, they are still considered <u>phrases</u> because the noun before the *who*, *which*, or *that* does not have its own verb. These phrases modify nouns in sentences:

   People *who are happy* often have creative hobbies.

   My brother has many habits *which annoy me*.

   The dog *that lives next door* is friendly to everyone.

Exercise 2

Which of the following groups of words are phrases? Which are clauses? Label each one. Review the previous page if you have difficulty.

	Examples:	hoping to catch the bus	phrase
		she ran down the street, hoping to catch the bus	clause
		the man who lives next door	phrase
		she met the man who lives next door	clause

1. thinking about how to pass the course

2. he stayed up all night, thinking about how to pass the course

3. students were lying all over the grass

4. my girlfriend loves me

5. the girl who loves me

6. rear tires spinning and engine roaring

7. a trait that I share with many others

8. the desk near the window

9. he has a favorite place to study, the desk near the window

10. she was waiting by the cafe

11. her friend standing in the corner

12. the book that I bought yesterday

13. cruising down Market Street in his Porsche

14. the man that I married

15. he is my best friend, the man that I married

16. her hair blowing in the wind

17. she cruised down Market Street in her convertible, her hair blowing in the wind

18. a world in which no one listens to anybody else

Two Kinds of Clauses

You now know what a clause is, but there are two kinds of clauses you need to know about: **dependent** and **independent**. To see the difference between the two kinds, read the examples below:

1. Mary likes the clown. (independent clause)

2. *because* Mary likes the clown (dependent clause)

Words like *because* are called **subordinators**. When we use a subordinator at the beginning of a clause, the clause becomes dependent (or subordinate) and can no longer stand alone as a sentence. Dependent clauses (subordinate clauses) should always be attached to independent clauses.

Examples: *Because* Mary likes the clown, she goes to the circus often. = sentence
          dependent clause   +   independent clause

           Mary goes to the circus often *because* she likes the clown. = sentence
          independent clause   +   dependent clause

Some Common Subordinators

as	wherever	as if
as long as	while	as though
as soon as	though	because
after	although	since
before	even though	so that
by the time	even if	that
until	if	who/whom
when	unless	whose
whenever	whether	which

Remember: When we join two logically-related ideas with subordinators, the two ideas must be in the same sentence.

Exercise 3

Identify the following as independent or dependent clauses.

Examples:	although the issue is complicated	D (Dependent)
	people have strong opinions	I (Independent)

---

1. whenever I feel bored

2. she proposed to me

3. although I am her cousin

4. Charles says he loves me

5. because I was tired

6. before the semester began

7. while I was sitting on the park bench

8. my roommate intends to finish college

9. after Arlene left for Chicago

10. wherever you may go

11. since Mary and Jack got married

12. many people hate to write

13. unless you stop doing that right now

14. even though Sherry knows

Fragments

Sentence fragments are phrases or dependent clauses punctuated as if they were complete sentences.

Exercise 4

In the exercise below, all of the groups of words are punctuated as complete sentences, but some are <u>dependent clauses</u>, so they are fragments. Identify each group of words as a sentence or a fragment.

Examples:	When I went to the bookstore.	fragment
	I went to the bookstore.	sentence

1. Since I had nothing else for lunch today except a hamburger.

2. If I could be alone to work on my homework.

3. She has been a nurse for ten years.

4. Because she's a wonderful person with all kinds of unusual talents.

5. While Mary loves chocolate.

6. Success comes to people who work hard.

7. Although I do not enjoy hard work.

8. When exams are just around the corner.

9. Because the afternoon was cold enough for a sweater.

10. I wish you would begin at the beginning of the story.

Exercise 5

In the following exercise, all of the groups of words are punctuated as sentences, but some are <u>phrases</u>, so they are fragments. Identify each group of words as a sentence or fragment.

Examples: The man in the checkered suit.   fragment

                    The man is wearing a checkered suit.   sentence

---

1.   Before the darkest part of the evening.

2.   A laboratory for the study of animal life in the South Pacific.

3.   We all worked on making the lunch for the whole group.

4.   Many times in the past, I have gone to his parties.

5.   Enjoyable, crowded parties with good music, many people, and wonderful food and wine.

6.   Such as snakes, rats, and insects.

7.   For example, the ugly car that he drives.

8.   He became bored during the lecture.

9.   His eyes staring vacantly ahead.

10.   Good friends all the way through college, both in San Francisco and Los Angeles.

Exercise 6

In each of the following pairs, underline the fragment.

Examples: Marian bought a lottery ticket.   <u>Hoping to win a million dollars</u>.

Marian bought a lottery ticket.   <u>Because she wanted to win a million dollars</u>.

---

1.   College is much more difficult than high school. Even though students spend fewer hours in class every day.

2.   I dislike teachers who grade unfairly. Especially those who give higher grades to their favorite students.

3.   Helen studies at least five hours every day. Always trying to keep up her g.p.a.

4.   Because most people who watch MTV on a regular basis are very young. Performers such as Frank Sinatra and Peggy Lee do not appear on this music channel.

5.   I study on weekends. Because on weekdays, I work at a cafe after school.

6.   I am taking a number of difficult courses this semester. For example, Spanish, economics, and microbiology.

7.   I only sleep four hours a night. Which is not enough sleep for me to feel rested the next day.

8.   I am majoring in business. A very difficult and time-consuming major.

What do you notice about the position of most of the fragments in relation to the sentences? Most fragments follow the sentences to which they should be attached. Some people automatically put a period at the end of each sentence. Without waiting until they decide whether they want to add more to the sentence. In doing so, they often create a fragment--as I just did. Can you spot it? Identify it by underlining it.

Because most fragments follow the sentences to which they should be attached, they are easy to correct. Simply join them to the sentences they follow.

Exercise 7

Now go back and correct the sentences in Exercise 6.

Examples: Marion often goes to Las Vegas, hoping to win a million dollars.

Marion often goes to Las Vegas because she wants to win a million dollars.

Proofreading for Fragments:

1.   Read your writing out loud, stopping at each period. Often you can hear that something is incomplete.

2.   Proofread by looking at every group of words that begins with a capital letter and ends with a period.

If a <u>subordinator</u> begins a sentence, check to make sure that the subordinate or dependent clause is joined to an independent clause. Subordinators must join two logically-related ideas into one sentence.

If there is no subordinator in the sentence, check to make sure the sentence has a subject-verb unit. If it doesn't, it is a phrase and should most likely be joined to either the previous sentence or the next sentence.

2. Run-Together Sentences

Run-together sentences occur when two sentences are joined with no punctuation between them or with only a comma connecting them.

Examples of run-together sentences: It was raining I got wet.
It was raining, I got wet.

Even though these thoughts go together logically, they are two separate sentences grammatically. A sentence can have two subjects and two verbs only if they are joined in some way. This unit explains some of the ways to join sentences.

Suggestions for fixing run-together sentences

Use a coordinator:

If the two sentences go together logically, often you should use a joining word to indicate the logical connection. This helps your reader to understand how your ideas relate to each other. One way of showing how the sentences are related is to join them with coordinators (remember them with the acronym **FANBOYS**):

For (cause)
And (addition)
Nor (addition of negatives)
But (opposition)
Or (alternatives)
Yet (opposition--same as but)
So (result)

Corrected run-together sentence: It was raining, so I got wet.

****Notice that a comma comes before the coordinator.

Exercise 1

In the exercise below, use one of the seven coordinators (**FANBOYS**: *for, and, nor, but, or, yet, so*) to join the sentences.

Example: I hate to see animals in cages, I don't like to go to the zoo.
Correct: I hate to see animals in cages, *so* I don't like to go to the zoo.

_____

1. Nick and Fran enjoyed the movie, they wished the seats had been more comfortable.

2. The TV wasn't working, I walked over to a friend's house to watch the game.

3. Fred remembered to get the hot dogs he forgot to buy the rolls.

4. The telephone was ringing, someone was at the front door as well.

5. Brett moved from Boston to Los Angeles, she wanted to get as far away as possible from her ex-husband.

6. On sunny days, I like to ride my bike in the park, I take a walk on the beach.

7. There were not that many good jobs on campus, I took one at the mall.

8. Most of the class thought the main character was mean, I thought he was misunderstood.

Use a Subordinator

You can also show the relationship between two sentences by using **a subordinator** to change one of the sentences into a dependent clause.

Corrected run-together sentences: *Since* it was raining, I got wet.
I got wet *because* it was raining.

**** When a subordinator comes in the beginning of a sentence, put a comma after the clause it is attached to. If the subordinator comes in the middle of the sentence, do not use a comma.

While there are too many subordinators to list, here are some common ones:

Time words: after, before, since, when, while, as, whenever, until, by the time, as soon as, until, as long as,

Cause-effect words: because, since, as

Opposition words: while, whereas, although, though, even though

Condition words: if, unless, even if, whether

You will notice that some of these words (*since, as, while*) have more than one meaning. Because these words can express more than one logical relationship, it is important to use them carefully so that your reader will not be confused.

14

Exercise 2

In the following sentences, correct the run-together sentences by adding an appropriate subordinator. You will find a list of subordinators on the previous page.

Example: Marge was an "A" student, she didn't have to worry about her English midterm.
Correct: *Since* Marge was an "A" student, she didn't have to worry about her English midterm.

Example: Juan likes to read the newspaper, he wants to know what is going on in the world.
Correct: Juan likes to read the newspaper *because* he wants to know what is going on in the world.

---

1. Serana likes action movies, Theresa likes comedies.

2. Harry was a good musician, he never could keep a steady job in a band.

3. Gloria knew all the ropes, she met Peter.

4. The sunshine in March was pleasant, it was a disaster for local farmers.

5. Sue would buy a new car, she had the money.

6. I missed the 8 am bus, I slept through my alarm.

7. We decided to leave the park, it started to rain.

8. The committee members looked over the application, they were pleased with the candidate's responses.

Use a semicolon or a period

You can, of course, always use a semicolon to join run-together sentences or a period to separate them into two sentences.

Corrected run-together sentences: It was raining. I got wet.
It was raining; I got wet.

But when possible, it is better to use a joining word--a coordinator or a subordinator--to show the logical connection between sentences, so that you give your reader more information about how your sentences relate. Always look first to see if the logical connection can be expressed with a coordinator or subordinator. If not, semicolons are useful for joining sentences that seem to belong together, but are not related in ways easily expressed by coordinators or subordinators.

Exercise 3

Insert a semicolon where the sentences run together.

---

1. The tide had risen three feet by nightfall, waves began to lap across the top of the pier.

2. Something was obviously wrong with the meatloaf, it was glowing in the dark.

3. Mike never heard the third-base coach screaming for him to stop he was out at home plate by ten feet.

4. Our manager proposed a ten percent reduction in salaries the staff did not like the idea.

5. I was happy with my new apartment, it was in a good location and the rent was very low.

A final note on run-togethers:

<u>Beware</u>: Transition words like *however, then, therefore, moreover, for example*, **DO NOT** join sentences. You still need a semicolon or a period if you use them between sentences.

Incorrect: It was raining therefore I got wet.

Correct: It was raining; therefore, I got wet.
    It was raining. Therefore, I got wet.

The problems with transition words are that you have to remember to use a semi-colon or a period between sentences and that they are over-used and clunky. Frequently, you can use a coordinator to mean the same thing and to connect your ideas more smoothly. Try using *but* instead of *however, so* instead of *therefore* or *then*, and *and* instead of *moreover*.

MAN HING MARKET - CLEMENT

Exercise 4

Correct the following run-together sentences below. Here are the most common ways to correct them:

Example of a run-together sentence: I ran all the way to the corner, I still missed my bus.

Best choice: I ran all the way to the corner, but I still missed my bus.
Although I ran all the way to the corner, I still missed my bus.

Using **a joining word** is the best choice because it lets your reader know the logical connection between your two sentences. In this case, the logical connection is opposition.

Alternative choice: I ran all the way to the corner; I still missed my bus.
Only use a semicolon when you cannot find a joining word that works.

Least preferable choice: I ran all the way to the corner. I still missed my bus.
By using a period, you are giving your reader even less information about how the sentences relate.

---

1.   The Navajos are a nomadic people, the Hopis are farmers.

2.   Despite my father's plans for me, I didn't want to study medicine, I wanted to become a teacher.

3.   Elaine was very ill, she missed three days of class.

4.   The Student Union doesn't have enough tables, many students are forced to eat outside.

5.   Bishop Tutu spoke about the problems in South Africa, he stressed the need for speedy solutions to those problems.

6.   The book has been on the best-seller list for months, it's one of the most boring novels I've ever read.

7.   In an earthquake, buildings sway back and forth, many rattle and groan.

18

Exercise 5

Using the directions from exercise 4, correct the following run-together sentences.

___

1. Billie Holliday was one of the greatest jazz singers of all time, she captivated audiences wherever she went.

2. Mark is not very interested in sports, he does, however, like to water-ski.

3. My living room is very small, I should not buy any more furniture.

4. Some students graduate from high school without having learned much of anything, nobody knows exactly whose fault this is.

5. Dedicated ecologists do not kill wildlife, they shoot with cameras instead of guns.

6. Some people are very considerate, others think of nobody but themselves.

7. I can't wait for my mid-terms to be over, then I can finally get some sleep.

8. Jean is my best friend, she is always there for me when I need her.

9. She is not only an excellent student, she is also an outstanding athlete.

10. The room was filthy, empty beer cans and half-eaten food were scattered all over the floor.

Exercise 6

Now that you have fixed some run-togethers in isolated sentences, see if you can find the run-togethers in this paragraph. Correct any you find using the directions from exercise 4. If you have difficulty, try reading the passage out loud.

Sleep is a subject we should all know a lot about, we spend one third of our lives sleeping. Even though everyone sleeps, scientists have only recently begun to understand what goes on when we sleep. They used to believe that the body repairs itself while asleep, there is some truth to this but the body also does this while awake. The brain does not simply shut itself off at night, it goes through a complicated series of chemical changes. Scientists have begun to chart these changes, working with complex instruments that measure brain-wave patterns. They have found that we do not move smoothly from being awake to being asleep, we pass through a cycle of four sleep stages. At each stage blood pressure and pulse rate drop, the body temperature also goes down. In the second stage the number and length of brain waves go up, while the sleeper's eyes begin to move rapidly back and forth behind their lids. Scientists call this activity rapid eye movements, or REMs, the activity that accompanies most of our dreaming. If a person is deprived of REM sleep, that person will soon become bad-tempered and irritable. A full night's sleep is not a single, unbroken state but consists of four or five of these multi-stage sleep cycles.

Exercise 7

Some of the sentences in this paragraph are run-togethers. Review the information in this chapter and correct any run-together sentences that you find.

In 1867, a chef at a hotel in Saratoga Springs accidentally dropped some thinly sliced potatoes into hot cooking oil, instantly the world found a new delicacy: the potato chip. At the time, Saratoga Springs was America's most fashionable resort, fads that started there usually found immediate success. Almost overnight, the potato chip became Saratoga's hottest item. The wide, tree-lined avenues were filled with people eating potato chips, the huge veranda of the United States Hotel was no different; it was filled with chip-eaters too. Some of the richest, most powerful people in the world consumed them regularly, for instance, the Vanderbilts could often be seen daintily plucking chips from paper cups on their stroll back to their mansion. The elegant "Saratoga chips" remained the delicacy of the wealthy until 1925, when the first chip factory was constructed in Albany, New York. The potato chip was no longer the snack of only the rich and famous, it became a common household item. Of course potato chips have changed a great deal in the last hundred years, now they come in various textures and flavors, some even come stacked in paper tubes! Still, the next time you grab a handful of greasy, flavor-dusted chips, you might pause to remember the noble origins of that humble food. It might be the closest you'll ever get to living like the Vanderbilts, you'd better enjoy it!

Proofreading Tips

a) Read your essay out loud after you have printed it out. Often, you can catch run-together sentences by hearing where you paused and needed to start a new sentence.

b) If run-together sentences continue to be a problem for you, try circling every comma in your essay (or have the computer search out the commas for you). Then check to see if you have a sentence both before <u>and</u> after the comma. If you do, you will need to fix it by joining the sentences with a coordinator, subordinator or semi-colon or by separating them with a period.

GREEN APPLE BOOKS – CLEMENT

3. Subject-Verb Agreement

When we write in the present tense, the verbs have to agree with their subjects. Notice the difference in the verbs in these two lists:

I	live in the desert.	He	live<u>s</u> in the desert.
You	live in the desert.	She	live<u>s</u> in the desert.
They	live in the desert.	It	live<u>s</u> in the desert.

If the subject of a present tense verb is a third-person singular pronoun--*he*, *she*, or *it*, (or any noun these pronouns can replace)--the verb must have an *-s* ending. All other noun or pronoun subjects do not have verbs with *-s* endings.

We make subject-verb agreement errors when we leave out *-s* endings on present tense verbs with singular third person subjects, or when we add *-s* endings to present tense verbs with plural subjects (or the subjects *I* and *you*).

Finding Subject-Verb Agreement Errors:

To find subject-verb agreement errors, you should know (a) how to identify subject-verb units in sentences and (b) how to identify singular and plural noun subjects.

a.   **To find subject-verb units, follow these two steps:**

1.   <u>First, find the verb, by using the time test.</u>

Change the time (or tense) of the sentence to another time:

from:	The plant <u>grows</u> well in the desert.	(now)
to:	The plant <u>grew</u> well in the desert.	last year, or 20 years ago)
OR:	The plant <u>will grow</u> well in the desert.	(next month or next year)

The verb shows the time or tense in a sentence; since we changed *grows* to *grew* or *will grow* when we changed the time, *grows* is the verb.

2.   <u>Once you have found the verb, it's easy to find the subject.</u>

Ask yourself: Who or what <u>*grows*</u> ?
                                                    verb

The answer is *plant*, so *plant* is the subject of the verb *grows,* and we call *plant grows* a subject-verb unit.

b. **To decide whether a noun subject is singular or plural**, try replacing the noun subject of your sentence with a pronoun.

If the noun subject can be replaced with the 3rd person singular pronoun *he*, *she*, or *it*, the present tense verb must have an *-s* ending:

> (*It*)
> The plant grow<u>s</u> well in the desert.

If the noun subject can be replaced with the 3rd person plural pronoun *they*, or the pronoun *we*, the verb does not have an *-s* ending:

> (*They*)
> The plants grow well in the desert.

So check for subject-verb agreement in this way:

Example sentence: Charles rides the bus every day.

a.   <u>Identify the subject-verb unit by following the two-step process:</u>

> 1.   To find the verb, we change the time or tense of the sentence.
>
>   Charles rode the bus every day last year.
>
>   We changed *ride* to *rode*, so *ride* is the verb.
>
> 2.   To find the subject, ask yourself, who or what *rides*?
>   The answer is *Charles*, so *Charles* is the subject of the verb *rides*.

b.   <u>Replace the noun subject *Charles* with the appropriate pronoun:</u>

> [Charles = he]   He rides the bus every day.

Since *he/she/it* subjects must have *-s* endings in the present tense, *he rides* is correct, so we can say that the subject and verb agree.

Reminder: The plural pronoun *they* refers to people <u>and</u> things.

Example: My aunts live next door.   *They* often visit my family.
> (The pronoun *they* refers to the plural noun *aunts*.)

Example: The trees need watering.   *They* also need fertilizer.
> (The pronoun *they* refers to the plural noun *trees*.)

Exercise 1

Column A is a list of subject nouns. First substitute the appropriate pronoun for the subject noun and write it in column B. Then, using the verb in parentheses, make the correct subject-verb combination.

	A	B	(verb)	S/V
Ex.	John	he	(walk)	John walks.
1.	girl	_____	(know)	_____
2.	children	_____	(sing)	_____
3.	tree	_____	(grow)	_____
4.	king	_____	(rule)	_____
5.	Chris and I	_____	(talk)	_____
6.	Sarah	_____	(live)	_____
7.	stove	_____	(heat)	_____
8.	wheels	_____	(turn)	_____
9.	brother	_____	(play)	_____
10.	paintings	_____	(hang)	_____

Exercise 2

In each sentence, fill in the bracket above the noun subject with the appropriate pronoun; then fill in the blank with the correct <u>present tense</u> form of the given verb.

Example: [He]
John <u>drinks</u> wine with every meal.   (DRINK)

---

1.   [   ]
     My plant _____ lots of sunlight.   (GET)

2.   [   ]
     Mrs. Johnson _____ on buying the tickets.   (INSIST)

3.   [   ]
     Most Americans _____ television every day.   (WATCH)

4.   [   ]
     My son and I _____ the neighbors who moved.   (MISS)

5.   [   ]
     Bob _____ his job difficult.   (FIND)

6.   [   ]
     The flowers _____ droopy.   (LOOK)

7.   [   ]
     Sally _____her two dogs daily.   (WALK)

8.   [   ]
     The newspaper article _____ me.   (CONFUSE)

9.   [   ]
     Mary and I _____ weightlifters.   (ADMIRE)

10. [   ]
     Mr. Martin _____ novels.   (WRITE)

Exercise 3

Fill in the appropriate present tense form of the given verb.

1)   If the subject is singular (can be replaced by *he*, *she* or *it*), the verb has an *-s* ending.

      Example: EAT   Joan <u>eats</u> a burrito every day.

2)   If the subject is plural (can be replaced by *they*) or *I* or *you*, the present tense verb has no *-s* ending.

      Example: EAT   Joan and her boyriend <u>eat</u> burritos every day.

---

1. HOPE   My sister _____to become a special education teacher.

2. SAY   I always _____ what I think.

3. RUN   Every morning, Chris and Peter _____ four miles.

4. ENJOY Most of the time, Juan _____ his work.

5. FRY*   Ginger always _____ eggs until they are as hard as rocks.

6. TAKE   Medical careers _____ a lot of training.

7. SAY   The sign _____ that the store will open at noon.

8. SEE   My sister and I usually _____ our parents once a month.

9. SEEM   New styles often _____ strange at first.

10. MARRY If she _____ him, will they stop fighting?

*If a verb ends in consonant + *y*, change the *y* to *ie* before adding *s*, e.g. *cry* -->--> *cries.*

Exercise 4

The following sentences are all in present tense. Correct any subject-verb agreement errors and remember to use present tense in your corrections. (Not every verb needs changing.)

    incorrect: My class seem difficult.

This sentence has a subject-verb agreement error because the subject *class* is singular (can be replaced by *it*), so the verb should have an -*s* ending.

    correct: My class seem<u>s</u> difficult.

_____

1.   Every year my husband surprise me on my birthday.

2.   Jennifer take her children to school every morning at 8:00.

3.   I think the movie sound scary.

4.   Shirley live in a small town near Chicago.

5.   My sisters all loves chocolate ice cream.

6.   They risk a finc by driving so fast.

7.   The trains goes to St. Louis every day at noon.

8.   My personal trainer work at a local college.

9.   The weather report looks depressing.

10.   He think we should buy a new car.

One Source of Difficulty: Which has the error, the subject or the verb?

Sometimes when we discover a subject-verb agreement error, we immediately assume that the error is in the verb. For instance, in the following sentence:

(incorrect)   Many teacher assign a lot of homework

we can see that the subject *teacher* is singular (can be replaced by the pronoun *she* or *he*), and so we try to make the subject and verb agree by adding an -*s* ending to the verb. But the sentence isn't about just *one teacher*, but about *many teachers*. So the subject needs the plural -*s* ending; the verb is correct:

(correct)   Many teacher<u>s</u> assign a lot of homework.

Exercise 5

The following sentences all contain subject-verb agreement errors. Identify the subject-verb unit in each sentence, and ask yourself if the subject <u>or</u> the verb is incorrect; add an -*s* ending wherever appropriate. (Note that modifiers like *many, all, several, a few,* and *some* indicate that the count noun should have a plural -*s* ending.)

incorrect: My classmate all speak more than one language.

correct: My classmate<u>s</u> all speak more than one language.

---

1.   One neighborhood cafe serve free coffee before 7 a.m.

2.   Many student work on research projects together.

3.   Tonight the Elton John concert begin at 8:00.

4.   Most teenager grow tired of school in the senior year.

5.   In the United States, many mother work full-time.

6.   My employer provide health insurance for permanent employees of the company.

7.   A local artist paint watercolors of her garden in bright primary colors.

8.   Our team's shortstop never get a hit.

A Second Source of Difficulty: Non-Count Noun Subjects

Many nouns in English are non-count; we can't count them by saying *two homeworks*, *three advices*, or *four informations*. No matter how much we are referring to, we never add *-s* endings to non-count nouns.

When non-count nouns are subjects, they are just like singular subjects; their present tense verbs have *-s* endings.

Correct Examples:

This week's *homework* seem<u>s</u> very difficult	(*Homework* can refer to many assignments, or just one.)
Your *advice* help<u>s</u> me a lot.	(You may have given me one suggestion or a lot of *advice*.)
The new *equipment* work<u>s</u> well.	(*Equipment* can refer to one piece of equipment or more than one.)
The *evidence* show<u>s</u> his guilt.	(*Evidence* can refer to one piece of evidence or more.)

See Unit 5--Singular and Plural Nouns-- for a list of commonly-used non-count nouns.

Exercise 6

In the following sentences, you will look at both the subject and the verb to correct subject-verb agreement errors. All of the sentences have subject-verb agreement errors.

Examples:

incorrect: My homeworks take a lot of time.

correct: My **homework takes** a lot of time.

incorrect: Many musician plays more than one instrument.

correct: Many **musicians play** more than one instrument.

incorrect: My oldest sister eat all the time.

correct: My oldest **sister eats** all the time.

---

1.   John play soccer every day after school.

2.   The evidences seems valid to me.

3.   Some mother takes their children to daycare every day before work.

4.   Children's Playgrounds is the oldest playground in the United States.

5.   Some midterms is more difficult than final exams.

6.   Our Student Union do not provide many places to meet people.

7.   My backpack carry all of my books and supplies.

8.   The child play with her toys.

9.   Most teacher helps you with your assignments.

10.   Teenager often longs for freedom.

Another Source of Difficulty: sentences often have more than one subject and verb.

<u>Sentences often have more than one verb</u>:

Example: Stan plays piano and sings in the church choir.

To find the verbs, apply the time test; change the time or tense of the sentence:

(Last year)   Stan <u>played</u> piano and <u>sang</u> in the church choir.

To change the time, we had to change *plays* to *played* and *sings* to *sang*. Since verbs are words that change to show time, both *plays* and *sings* are verbs in this sentence.

To find the subject, we ask who *plays* and *sings*? The answer is *Stan*, so *Stan* is the subject of the verbs *plays* and *sings*. And since *Stan* is a noun that can be replaced by the singular pronoun *he*, the singular subject and *-s* ending verbs agree.

<u>Verbs can have more than one subject</u>:

Example: Stan and his brother play piano and sing in the church choir.

If we ask who *plays* and *sings*, the answer is *Stan* and *his brother*, so both *Stan* and *his brother* are subjects of the verbs *play* and *sing*. And since the subjects *Stan* and *brother* can be replaced by the plural pronoun *they*, the verbs don't have *-s* endings.

<u>Many sentences have more than one subject-verb unit</u>:

Example: Stan plays piano, but his sister knows very little about music.

To find the verbs, change the time:

(Last year)   Stan <u>played</u> piano, but his sister <u>knew</u> very little about music.

The words we changed are *plays* and *knows*, so both are verbs in the sentence.

To find the subject, ask yourself:

Who *plays piano*? The answer is *Stan*, so *Stan* is the subject of the verb *plays*.

Who *knows little about music*? The answer is *sister*, so *sister* is the subject of the verb *knows*.

So the example sentence has two subject-verb units: *Stan plays* and *sister knows*.

Exercise 7

The following sentences are all in the present tense. Correct any subject-verb agreement errors that you find. Watch for more than one subject and verb in the sentences.

Example: incorrect: Juan live in Pacifica and work in San Francisco.

            correct: Juan **lives** in Pacifica and **works** in San Francisco.

---

1.   The disc-jockey play rock records and announces upcoming concerts.

2.   In the morning Gretchen and Paul exercises and in the afternoon she sing while he plays piano.

3.   That television announcers speaks with a Texas accent, but his assistant speak with a New York accent.

4.   My husbands own a motorcycle, but he prefers to drive his car.

5.   My roommate listen to the radio all the time, even when she study.

6.   Antiques increases in value every year.

7.   My apartments rent for twice as much this year even though the landlord never fix anything.

8.   The building need lots of repairs, but my brother and his wife wants to buy it.

9.   Bob act stupid when he and his buddies drinks too much.

10. Judy's CD collection impresses all of her guests, but she don't listen to music.

Exercise 8

1. Underline each verb in the following paragraph.

2. Rewrite the paragraph, changing "Andy and Oscar" to "Oscar," and making whatever changes are necessary.

The first sentence will begin like this: *After leaving Chicago, Oscar now <u>lives</u> on a farm because he <u>wants</u>*. . . .

After leaving Chicago, Andy and Oscar now live on a farm because they want a quiet life in the fresh air. They get up every morning at dawn and before breakfast pick their way through the cow dung, open the smelly chicken coop, and hold their noses as they snatch an egg. While making a fire in their woodburning stove, they choke on the smoke. Then Andy and Oscar drive a deafening tractor out to the field, where, as they fill their lungs with the blowing dust, they sneeze furiously. Until late in the evening, they do chores in the barn. Exhausted, they fall asleep and dream of a sound-proof office and an air-conditioned room.

Special Verbs:

1.   The verb *HAVE*: To make the verb *have* agree with a *he/she/it* subject in the present tense, we change the spelling:

   Example: [*She*]   [*They*]
   Mary *has* a cat, but her parents *have* a dog.

In the present tense if the subject is a singular noun or pronoun,(*he,she*,or *it*), use *has*.

If the subject is a plural noun, or the pronoun *they*, *I*, *you*, or *we*, use *have*.

2.   The verb *BE*: The verb *BE* is unusual, because it agrees with its subject in both present and past tense.

Present:	**Past:**
I *am* a student.	I *was* a student.
You *are* a student.	You *were* a student.
They *are* students.	They *were* students.
We *are* students.	We *were* students.
He *is* a student.	He *was* a student.
She *is* a student.	She *was* a student.

Exercise 9

Read the following paragraph and correct any subject-verb agreement errors.

   My sister live on the ground floor of a two-story apartment and hates living there. For one thing, many cat in her neighborhood howls right below her bedroom window all night and knock over her garbage cans. One cat waits patiently outside her door until she open it and then pounce on her feet, ruining her stockings. But the people living upstairs is even worse than the cats. The mother starts a fire almost every month because she forget to turn off the stove when she leave the kitchen, and the daughter faithfully practices her gymnastics every evening just as my sister sit down to study. Even more annoying, the fathers park his car in my sister's parking space and peek in every time he go past her front window, so she always have to keep her curtains closed. All in all, living there has not been a pleasant experience for my poor sister.

Proofreading for Subject-Verb Agreement Errors:

1. Read your work out loud; often you can hear an incorrect -*s* ending, or notice that an -*s* ending is missing.

2. Follow the two-step process for identifying verbs and subjects, and then look carefully at present tense subject-verb units.

3. Check both the subject and the verb. An error could be in either one.

4. Make sure that plural noun subjects (or the pronouns *I*, *you*, *we*, and *they*) have verbs without -*s* endings.

5. Make sure that singular subjects (*he/she/it*, or nouns these pronouns can substitute for) have -*s* ending verbs.

MAIN GATE - JAPANESE TEA GARDEN
GOLDEN GATE PARK 金門公園

4. Other Kinds of Subject-Verb Agreement

In this chapter, we will look at some of the subject-verb agreement problems that give students the most trouble. But first, here is a brief description of how to find the subject and verb in a sentence.

First, find the verb. While you may have heard that verbs are the action words, that is not always true. **Verbs are words that change their form to indicate the tense or time of a sentence.** Look at the following sentences:

> Swimming *is* my favorite sport.
> Swimming *was* my favorite sport.
> Swimming *will be* my favorite sport.
> Swimming and football *are* my favorite sports.

We would probably say that *swimming* is the action word in the sentence, but it is not the verb. <u>*Is* is the verb </u>because it changes with time or tense.

Now that you have found the verb, you can find the subject. **The subject is the word that answers the question who or what in relation to the verb.** Look at the following sentences.

> The storm rages in California. (What *rages?* The *storm* does, so the *storm* is the subject.)

> George is beating on the door. (Who *is beating* on the door? *George* is, so *George* must be the subject.)

> Regular lubrication and maintenance are necessary to keep a car in good shape. (What *are* necessary? *Regular lubrication and maintenance* are, so they must be the subjects.)

Now that you can identify the subject and verb in a sentence, you have to make sure that they agree. In the present tense, verbs agree with their subjects when they have the correct ending. If the subject is third person singular (*he-she-it*), the present tense verb must have an *-s* ending. With all the other subjects, the present tense verb does <u>not</u> need an *-s* ending.

Sources of Common Problems

While it is obvious that words like *dog* and *John* are singular, sometimes it is not so easy for us to see that a word is singular. The following is a list of common words that, when used as subjects, are singular and in the same class as *he-she-it* subjects.

each	anything	everybody
either	someone	everything
neither	somebody	no one
another	something	nobody
anyone	one	nothing
anybody	everyone	

So this sentence is **incorrect:**   Nobody like these donuts.

This is **correct:**   Nobody *likes* these donuts.

Exercise 1

Correct the following subject-verb agreement errors.

> Example: Everything in the store are on sale.
> **Correct:** Everything in the store *is* on sale.

---

1. Each brother like potato chips.

2. Everybody know that too much fat is bad for you.

3. Neither sister drive a car to get to school.

4. Everyone watch the news in my dorm.

5. Somebody need to walk the dog to the park.

6. Each individual have a different way of dealing with stress.

There + "to be"

Look at the following sentence:

correct: There *are* four apples on the table.

If the verb is *are,* how do we find the subject? Ask yourself *who* or *what* are (on the table)? You will come up with *apples* as a subject, and this is correct.

The problem with this kind of sentence is that a writer frequently begins a sentence with "There is" (or "There was"), which is singular, and follows it with a plural subject.

incorrect: There *is* four apples on the table.

Even though the subject comes after the verb in this type of sentence, the subject and verb must still agree.

Exercise 2

Correct the following subject-verb agreement errors.

Example: There was many problems with the new boss.
Correct: There **were** many problems with the new boss.

---

1. There is several characters in this story.

2. There was many ways to solve the problem, but the board took no action.

3. In her family, there is two brothers and a sister.

4. Last spring, there was several kinds of flowers in his garden.

5. There has been many interpretations of this book.

6. There is many reasons why it is hard to find a good job.

7. In my old neighborhood, there was many homeless people.

Separated Subject and Verb

The trickiest part about identifying subjects comes when there is more than one noun in front of the verb. Look at the following sentences:

correct: The sweaters in the drawer are made of wool.

Here, answering the *who* or *what* question (what are made of wool?) tells us that *sweaters* is the subject. But sometimes the *who* or *what* question does not give us enough information:

correct: The holes in the sweater are going to be fixed.

Here answering the who or what question does not give us an answer (both *holes* and *sweater* make sense here). So we have to remember another rule:

Nouns that follow prepositions cannot be subjects.

Prepositions are words like *in, of, at, by, from, on, by* and nouns that follow them cannot be the subject of the sentence. Actually you do not really need to memorize this rule because you already know it . Here is an example:

incorrect: Of the sweater is pretty.
What? Does that make sense? Since *of*, which is a preposition, comes in front of the noun *sweater*, it cannot be the subject. Because sentences need subjects and this sentence does not have one, the sentence does not make sense. What you meant to write was:
correct: The sweater is pretty.

So be careful and <u>reread your sentences from the beginning</u> to make sure that the verb agrees with the subject.

Exercise 3

In the following sentences, the subject is not always right next to the verb or verbs. To make sure you have the correct subject, read the whole sentence out loud, following the steps for identifying subjects and verbs. Correct the errors in agreement that you find.

Example: Paul, unlike his friends, believe different things, and hold different ideas.
Correct: Paul, unlike his friends, **believes** different things, and **holds** different ideas.

---

1. I think the commercials on television is stupid.

2. Each of you students have the power to change your life.

3. One of the reasons are his parents' wealth.

4. My paper on the governments of three countries were very interesting.

5. After school, the kids on my block watches television, or plays in the street.

6. The new rules and regulations of the university was very confusing.

7. The representatives of the student council values the input they get from other students.

8. The management style of many companies have an effect on the prices consumers pay.

Some of the/All of the

Some of and *all of* are tricky because they can come before both singular and plural nouns. Here, you do need to look at the prepositional phrase to determine if the noun there is singular or plural. For example:

All of the homework is useful.

We use the verb *is* in this sentence because *all of* is followed by *homework,* a singular noun. *All* may sound like a lot, but *homework* is the important word here, and no matter how much homework you have, it is still a singular word.

Some of the players are retiring.

Here we use the verb *are* because *some of* is followed by the plural noun *players*.

Exercise 4

Complete each sentence by first deciding if the noun in the prepositional phrase is singular or plural, and then choose a verb that agrees with the subject.
Example: Some of the homework _____.
Possible Answer: Some of the homework is fairly easy to do.

_____

1. Some of the advice _____.

2. All of the students _____.

3. Some of the people _____.

4. Some of the information _____.

5. All of the work _____.

6. All of the regulations _____.

Exercise 5

The sentences below contain all of the common subject-verb agreement problems discussed in this unit. Read the sentences out loud and correct any agreement problems you find. Review this chapter if you encounter difficulty.

---

1. Men and women with college degrees is supposed to get a job.

2. Yesterday, there was many delays on The Golden Gate Bridge.

3. A mountain of pressures are upon him.

4. The problems that he faces is giving him nightmares.

5. Everybody think this is going to be a great show.

6. There is four ways in which San Francisco is different from Los Angeles.

7. The number of people looking for apartments are staggering.

8. In my church choir, the age of singers range from fifteen to sixty.

9. Nobody in this room have to leave early.

Subject-Verb Agreement with Adjective Clauses

The words WHO, WHOM, WHICH, THAT, WHEN, and WHERE are often the first words of what we call adjective clauses. Like adjectives, adjective clauses modify nouns. **When a sentence contains an adjective clause, the verb in the adjective clause agrees with the noun the clause modifies.**

Example: My parents, who give me support, have helped me to do well in college.
In this sentence, *who* refers to *my parents*, so the verb *have* agrees in number with *parents*.

Example: I enjoy having friends like Rosa who come from different cultures than my own.
In this sentence, *who* refers to *friends,* so the verb *come* agrees in number with *friends*.

Exercise 6
Circle the correct verb in each of the following sentences.

---

1. My friends who (lives/live) in Daly City just bought a house.

2. The students in the front row who (is/are) always cracking jokes keep the rest of the class laughing.

3. The tourists I met at Coit Tower, who (was/were) dressed mostly in plaid, wanted to see a real hippie.

4. The restaurant down by the docks, which (serves/serve) great seafood, is closed Sundays.

5. My dogs are the only ones in the neighborhood who (does/do) not bark at the moon.

6. Matilda is a health food nut who (detests/detest) artificial sweeteners, food coloring and preservatives.

7. Tennis is a game which (requires/require) the right equipment as well as good eye-hand coordination and stamina.

Exercise 7

Correct any verbs that do not agree with their subjects.

> Example: Sarah is the only one of the players who hit home runs.
> **Correct: Sarah** is the only one of the players who **hits** home runs.

---

1. The mailwoman gave me my mail, which, unfortunately, were mostly bills.

2. People who says writing ability isn't important are kidding themselves.

3. I find it difficult to have patience with people who like to have their own way all the time.

4. The paintings near the snack bar, which depicts local tourist attractions, bored me.

5. In order to keep up with current events which influences our lives, we should read a newspaper or watch the news regularly.

6. Most people who live by themselves appreciate a home-cooked meal.

7. My favorite restaurants are hole-in-the-wall establishments run by families who treat their customers like friends and serves reasonably-priced, nutritious meals.

8. The typical American who live in the South speak more slowly than his northern counterpart.

Exercise 8

This passage contains many of the agreement problems you have gone over in this unit.   If you have difficulty, try reading the passage out loud and reviewing the information in this unit.

One of the biggest problems that I experience each semester are picking my classes, but after a few confusing days I usually manage to figure out a schedule. It's just that there is so many interesting classes to choose from that I end up with a long list of choices which I narrow down by looking at the days and times they are offered. I never take classes that is offered in the late afternoon or evening since I have a job which require me to work from 4:00 to 9:00 every night. I also try to choose classes taught by instructors who my friend say are enthusiastic teachers who likes their students because I know that I will learn best in a class with a good teacher. I also have several other considerations when making up my schedule. For example, many of my friend want to take classes together but I don't always like the classes they've chosen. I also have problems figuring out which classes fulfill G.E. requirements because there is so many rules to follow. Putting a class schedule together can be very frustrating, but once I have one figured out, I feel great because I know that I've arranged a workable schedule to get me through another semester of school, bringing me closer to my dream: graduation.

Exercise 9

The following passage contains some common subject-verb agreement errors. Find and correct the errors.

There is some very important decisions that everyone have to make while a student; one is the choice of major. Long ago, I thought of majoring either in computers or clinical science or both, because both of these field interests me, both are useful, and medical technology have many job openings. Actually, I would like to work in a hospital mainly for the satisfaction of helping people, but working with computers offer a lot of possibilities, too. Now that so many different kinds of computers are being made, they are becoming more and more useful. And because the price of computers are going down, more and more hospitals can afford them, which mean more and more potential job openings. Every doctor I know, whether a specialist or general practitioner, are using computers for many purposes, and medical technologists who works with them also uses computers for research. Each of these fields offer high starting salaries. All in all, I could do well in either field, but ideally I would like to work in a hospital that use computers frequently.

5. Singular and Plural Nouns

Count Nouns: Most nouns name something you can count; for example, if you buy a bag of peanuts, you can count each peanut in the bag--*one peanut*, *two peanuts*, *three peanuts*, and so on. We call nouns like *peanut* count nouns, and usually we add an -*s* ending to show more than one.

<u>Singular count nouns</u> refer to one person or thing while <u>plural count nouns</u> refer to more than one person or thing. We have several ways of making count nouns plural.

Some Rules for Forming Plurals:

(1)   To make a count noun plural, you can often just add an -*s* ending:

book	book<u>s</u>	horse	horse<u>s</u>
movie	movie<u>s</u>	student	student<u>s</u>

(2)   Most count nouns ending in *o*, *s*, *sh*, *ch*, and *x* add -*es* to form plurals:

potato	potato<u>es</u>	church	church<u>es</u>
class	class<u>es</u>	dish	dish<u>es</u>
box	box<u>es</u>		

(3)   Many count nouns ending in a consonant followed by *y* change the *y* to *i* and add -*es* to form plurals:

company	compan<u>ies</u>	library	librar<u>ies</u>
baby	bab<u>ies</u>	family	famil<u>ies</u>

(4)   Still other count nouns change form rather than just the ending:

man	m<u>e</u>n	woman	wom<u>e</u>n
child	child<u>ren</u>	wife	wi<u>ves</u>

To be sure that you are using the correct plural form, consult this list or a dictionary.

Exercise 1

Complete the following sentences, making any underlined singular nouns plural. Notice that modifiers like *many*, *most*, and *two*, signal the plural form of count nouns.

Example: The <u>student</u> studied for the history midterm.

Many <u>students</u> studied for the history midterm.

---

1.   I watched <u>a film</u> while I was sick.

      I watched several _____ while I was sick.

2.   <u>The library</u> has <u>a collection</u> of rare books.

      Most _____ have _____ of rare books.

3.   <u>The photographer</u> took shots of <u>a wolf</u> traveling in <u>a pack</u>.

      A team of _____ took shots of _____ traveling in _____.

4.   <u>The woman</u> ran a daycare center.

      The three _____ ran a daycare center together.

5.   I wrote <u>an essay</u> for my history class.

      I wrote many _____ for my history class.

6.   Maria ate <u>a</u> stuffed <u>tomato</u> for dinner.

      Maria ate two stuffed _____ for dinner.

Notice that the articles *a* and *an* and *the* are all used before singular nouns--*a society, a wolf, an essay, the woman*. But only the article *the* can be used before plural nouns.

The article *a* is used before words beginning with a <u>consonant sound</u>:

   a <u>d</u>og   a <u>u</u>niversity   a <u>c</u>ar   a <u>h</u>ouse

The article an is used before words beginning with a <u>vowel sound</u>:

   an <u>o</u>ctopus   an <u>o</u>ld man   an <u>u</u>mbrella   an <u>a</u>wful movie

Non-Count Nouns: Some nouns name things you <u>cannot</u> count, things you can only measure. For example, if you buy a pound of peanut butter, you can't count the peanut butter; you can only measure it in weight or quantity, like ounces or cups. We call words like *peanut butter* **non-count nouns** and we do not add -*s* endings to the noun, no matter how much of it we are referring to. As subjects of verbs, non-count nouns are just like singular nouns, so in the present tense, their verbs have -*s* endings.

The following is a list of commonly-used nouns which are almost always non-count:

admiration	foolishness	luck	propaganda
advice	fun	luggage	psychiatry
air	furniture	machinery	psychology
architecture	fusion	mail	rain
assistance	garbage	math	recreation
baggage	generosity	mathematics	relaxation
blame	gravity	merchandise	reliability
boredom	happiness	momentum	research
bravery	hardware	money	rice
bread	health	music	sadness
butter	heat	news	safety
chemistry	help	nonsense	salt
cheese	homework	objectivity	scenery
clothing	honesty	oxygen	shopping
comprehension	housework	participation	significance
conservation	housing	patience	slang
correspondence	ignorance	pay	sleet
courage	immigration	peace	snow
darkness	information	permission	software
economics	integration	physics	status
electricity	intelligence	poetry	superiority
enjoyment	irritability	pollution	survival
entertainment	isolation	postage	traffic
estimation	jargon	poverty	transportation
equipment	junk	precipitation	violence
ethics	knowledge	precision	wealth
evidence	laughter	prestige	weather
evolution	legislation	pride	wisdom
excitement	leisure	productivity	work
fame	literature	progress	(but *art works*)

Non-count nouns do not have plural -*s* endings and cannot be used with *a* or *an*; they can be used with *the*. For example, we can say:

> *The advice* he gave me was helpful.
> He gave me *some* good *advice.*
> I asked him for *advice.*

but not: The *advices* he gave me were helpful.
Please don't give me *an advice.*

Exercise 2

Here is a list of a few of the nouns that are always non-count. Use each in a sentence.
Do not add -s endings to non-count nouns.

Example: homework   <u>My homework takes a lot of time.</u>

1.   advice   _____

2.   equipment   _____

3.   evidence   _____

4.   furniture   _____

5.   homework   _____

6.   housework   _____

7.   information _____

8.   knowledge   _____

9.   mail   _____

10. patience   _____

11. research   _____

12. software   _____

13. work   _____

Special Pattern #1: The following one-word modifiers modify singular count nouns. When they come in front of nouns, the nouns do not have plural *-s* endings.

another	Henry ordered *another hamburger.*
one	She owns *one car.*
every	*Every student* in the class is a freshman.
each	The teacher learned the name of *each child.*
either	You can choose *either movie* to watch.
neither	*Neither boy* brought his book to class.

Special Pattern #2:

one of	2 or more
every one of	2 or more
each of	2 or more
either of	2 or more
neither of	2 or more

Examples:
One of my sisters lives in Texas.
Every one of my friends is coming to the party.
Each of my aunts has two children.
Either of the two books is worth reading.
Neither of the two films sounds worthwhile to me.

In Pattern #2, the nouns following *of* have *-s* endings because they refer to more than one--*two or more sisters*, *several friends*, *two or more aunts*, *two books*, and *two films*.

Notice the important difference between Pattern #1 and Pattern #2:

#1:   If the single word *another, one, every, each, either,* or *neither* comes before the count noun, <u>the noun is singular and does not have an *-s* ending</u>.

#2:   If the words *one of, every one of, each of, either of,* or *neither of* come before a count noun, <u>the noun is plural and must have an *-s* ending</u>.

An important sign of the difference is the word *of*.

Exercise 3

In the following sentences, correct any plural -*s* ending errors that you find. Watch for Special Pattern #1 and Special Pattern #2 discussed on the previous page.

Examples:	incorrect:	Every students got an A in the midterm.
	correct:	Every **student** got an A in the midterm.
	incorrect:	One of my aunt owns a Fiat.
	correct:	One of my **aunts** owns a Fiat.

---

1. One of my favorite movie is on television tonight.

2. Lois likes to dance with one of her old boyfriend.

3. Each students needs to do his part of the research project.

4. Each of the student is writing about an aspect of urban pollution.

5. Every one of my relative is coming to the family reunion.

6. Julie wants to buy another cars.

7. Neither of her old car runs any more.

8. You can choose either of the dessert.

9. You should wear one of your new shirt.

10. Every freshmen has to adjust to a new campus.

11. Every one of Jane's novel gets published.

12. I spent two hours cleaning each rooms.

Exercise 4

In the following exercise, you will practice the patterns we've covered so far. Correct any plural -*s* ending errors that you find. Add -*s* endings to count nouns that should be plural, and cross out -*s* endings on singular count nouns or non-count nouns.

incorrect: Many student in the class were doing their homeworks.

correct: Many **students** in the class were doing their **homework**.

---

1. University student usually work part-time.

2. Every teachers gave a lot of test last semester.

3. Adolescence is one of the most important period in our lives.

4. I enjoy many kind of entertainments.

5. I found a lot of informations about social problem in the library.

6. Maria has several pet--one dog, three birds and four hamster--and she takes good cares of each ones.

7. Both country have large population.

8. Carl needs new furnitures for his living room, but he doesn't want to spend a lot of money on more junks.

9. Student should evaluate their teachers because students are the one who know if their teacher are effective.

10. Most of my neighbor paved their driveway with stones.

11. One of my oldest friend arrives on Friday, and every times he comes, I'm happy to see him.

12. It's fun to do researches with another students.

13. Each computers is working, but we can't find the softwares we need.

14. Neither of my brother has a job, so they have to do all the houseworks.

Exercise 5

Correct the plural -*s* ending errors in the following paragraph. Add -*s* endings to some nouns that should be plural, and cross out -*s* endings on nouns that should be singular or non-count.

Some educators believe that reducing class size is just one small step toward improving elementary education while other believe that there is no evidences to show that reducing class size will improve students' performance. Some teachers feel that, with fewer student, they will be able to give more individual attentions to student who need help with homeworks and more individual help in laboratory classes like biology and chemistry. School administrator hope that the class-size reduction program will eventually affect all student in kindergarten through third grade, at every schools. But some teachers and administrator think that school will still have problems even if classes are small because school don't have the necessary equipments and trained teacher to provide good instruction.

Proofreading for Plural -*S* Ending Errors:

1. Read your work out loud, reading exactly what you have written. Often you'll hear an -*s* ending that shouldn't be there, or recognize that an -*s* ending is missing.

2. Look at the count nouns in your sentences. Ask yourself if you are referring to one person or thing, or more than one person or thing.

3. Check to make sure that you have **not** added -*s* endings to non-count nouns. Refer to the list of non-count nouns in this unit.

4. Look at each noun preceded by *one, another, each, every, either,* and *neither.* Make sure that the noun does **not** have an -*s* ending.

5. Look at each noun preceded by *one of, every one of, each of, either of* and *neither of.* Make sure that the noun has an -*s* ending.

AQUATIC PARK—FOOT OF HYDE STREET

6. Past Tense Verbs and Past Participles

Past Tense Verb Endings

The following passage is in the simple past tense. Underline the verbs in the sentences, and then circle the subjects. (See Unit 3 for help with identifying verbs and subjects.)

Last year Sherry lived at home and commuted to school. Because the buses were often late, she sometimes arrived late for classes and missed the beginning of several lectures. This annoyed her very much. Also, she often wanted to stay at school in the evening for movies and concerts, but her parents refused. They worried about her being on the bus after dark. Sherry's parents also showed their protectiveness in other ways. They allowed her to date only boys from church or from their neighborhood.

Sherry rebelled against these conditions during her sophomore year. Without the knowledge or permission of her parents, Sherry applied for a job at a Stonestown store, and she landed a position in the cosmetics department of a small department store. She rented a room near campus for $300 a month, but since the landlady didn't provide cooking facilities, Sherry ended up spending a lot of money on restaurants for every meal. Sherry's mother and father disapproved of her moving out, but they agreed to let Sherry go. Sherry escaped from her parents, but she worked such long hours to pay for her room and meals that she never found the time to go to a movie or a concert.

1. Find three combinations of singular subjects (*I-you-he-she-it*) and verbs (example: *Sherry lived*) and write them here:

2. Find three combinations of plural subjects (*we-they-you*) and verbs (example: *they agreed*) and write them here:

3. Is there any difference between the endings on verbs with singular subjects and the endings on verbs with plural subjects? _____

   What do the verbs have in common? _____

Regular Verbs:

If a verb is a **regular** verb, we add a *-d* or an *-ed* ending to show past tense, or to make the correct form after *have* or *has* (the past participle form).

Examples: Now that I'm in college, I <u>learn</u> something every day.   (present tense)
Yesterday, I <u>learned</u> about capitalism.   (past tense)
I <u>have learned</u> a lot this semester.   (*have* form)

Exercise 1

Fill in each blank with the correct past tense form of the verb given.

Example: PLAY We <u>played</u> baseball all afternoon.

FRY 1. We _____ the fish we caught over the open fire.

STUDY 2. All of us _____ hard for the chemistry exam.

CRY 3. Mary _____ on his shoulder all through the movie.

MARRY 4. She _____ him on Saturday and left the following Monday.

TRY 5. Although the tickets were sold out weeks in advance, John _____ to get in the concert by posing as a photographer.

SHOP 6. Anthony _____ for all his Christmas presents at the art fair last summer.

ADMIT 7. No one _____ that he was tired.

PLAN 8. Nancy and Jim _____ their divorce as if they were going on vacation.

TERRIFY 9. The fireworks _____ the younger children.

COMPILE 10. The teachers _____ the materials into a handbook.

Exercise 2

Rewrite the following sentences, changing the verbs from present to past tense so that they show the correct time or tense.

Example: I listen to the radio.

Yesterday, <u>I listened to the radio.</u>

_____

1.   Jane likes John.

When she was a child, _____

2.   Marie looks terrific in her yellow dress.

_____ <u>yesterday.</u>

3.   My grandparents live in San Jose.

Before they moved to San Francisco, _____

4.   Lucy plays tennis more often than Fred.

When they were roommates, _____

5.   After a victory, the quarterback talks to reporters.

After last week's victory, _____

6.   Usually women care for the children.

In the 1800s, _____

7.   Sam donates every spare cent to the San Francisco Zoo.

Last summer, _____

8.   The lawyers discuss the case.

After the trial, _____

9.   The dog growls at salesmen and snarls at Avon ladies.

Before he went to Obedience School, _____

_____

10.   Many students graduate from high school.

_____ last year.

ALERT: Though we can't hear the -d ending in speech, *supposed to* and *used to* always have a -d ending!

    Examples: She was supposed to show her identification.

               They used to go dancing every Friday night.

               I am supposed to be home in an hour.

               He is used to taking a walk after dinner.

Exercise 3

In each of the following sentences, underline any verbs that should have *-ed* or *-d* endings and supply the missing letters. Watch for time expressions (*last week, yesterday, years ago*) that indicate past time.

incorrect: The committee <u>vote</u> to adjourn yesterday.

correct: The committee <u>voted</u> to adjourn yesterday.

---

1.   The elephant ask Mary for a ride last week.

2.   Fred use to live in Berkeley when he was a college student.

3.   Kathy studied all the time and so she graduate from college last year.

4.   College students are suppose to attend every class meeting.

5.   Last Sunday, Laura listen to the drummers in the park.

6.   Until I started school, I work fifty hours a week and party the rest of the time.

7.   Finally Jan's cat return home.

8.   As soon as the cat returned, her dog, who is suppose to be man's best friend, disappear for three weeks.

9.   Several years ago, I witness a crime and identify the criminal.

10. Virginia serve us tacos for dinner, but she realize too late that she forgot to pick up a can of refried beans when she shop for groceries last week.

Irregular Verbs:

If a verb is **irregular,** we change its form, instead of adding an -ed ending, to show past tense or make the correct form after *have* or *has* (the past participle form).

> Example: Ken <u>takes</u> a test almost every week.   (present tense)
> Yesterday, he <u>took</u> a history test.   (past tense)
> He <u>has taken</u> many tests this semester.   (have form)

You know most of the past tense and *have* forms of irregular verbs, but if you are unsure of the correct past or *have* form of an irregular verb, you can look it up in a dictionary. Look up the base form; after the correct pronunciation of the word is given, you will see the verb information in bold type:

> (Base Form) (Past)   (Past Participle--*have* form) (Present Participle--*ing* form)
> **take**   **took**   **taken**   **taking**

Exercise 4

In the following exercise, all of the underlined verbs in the first sentence are irregular. Change the verbs first to simple past tense and then to the *have* form.

> Example: Diana <u>sings</u> in the church choir.
>
> Last year, Diana <u>sang</u> in the church choir.
>
> She <u>has sung</u> in the church choir since she was 11 years old.

---

1. Eric <u>takes</u> piano lessons.

    Eric _____ piano lessons last year.

    Eric <u>has</u>_____piano lessons since he was 10 years old.

2. I <u>know</u> how to repair transmissions.

    I _____ how to repair transmissions when I was a teenager.

    I <u>have</u>_____how to repair transmissions since I was 13 years old.

3. Tina <u>drives</u> to school every day.

Tina _____ to school every day last week.

Tina <u>has</u>_____ to school ever since she was a freshman.

4. My sister regularly <u>breaks</u> promises.

She _____ a promise to me yesterday.

She <u>has</u>_____ many promises to me over the years.

5. I <u>write</u> many essays for my history class.

Last week, I _____ a ten-page paper about Columbus.

I <u>have</u>_____ five essays since the semester began.

6. Matt <u>reads</u> as much as he can.

He _____ an entire novel yesterday.

He <u>has</u>_____ four novels since last Saturday.

7. The president often <u>flies</u> in his private jet.

Last week, he _____ to Florida.

He <u>has</u>_____ across the United States several times this year.

8. Katy and Kris <u>know</u> how to speak Spanish.

Katy and Kris _____ how to speak Spanish when they were children.

Katy and Kris <u>have</u>_____ how to speak Spanish for many years.

Other Uses of -Ed Endings

You know that we add -*ed* endings to regular verbs, or change the form of irregular verbs to show past tense. In the last exercise, you also practiced using the past participle after *have* or *has*. We also use -*ed* endings in two other patterns:

Pattern 1:   Verb forms following the helping verbs *be* and *get*.

Some verbs have two parts, first a helping verb--a form of *to be* or *to get*--and then a main verb. The main verb has an -*ed* or -*ed* ending (the past participle), no matter what tense the helping verb is.

Examples: a.   In my favorite restaurant, the meals *are served* quickly.

b.   Last year an award *was given* to the restaurant, and the chef *was thrilled* when his innovative recipes won the award.

c.   Laura *got bored* with her job as a secretary.

d.   Laura *was hired* by a restaurant.

e.   Now Laura *gets paid* very well for her work.

Reminder: In each of the sentences, the time of the action--the tense--is shown by the form of *to be* or *to get* (the helping verb). The main verb aways has a past participle ending: *are served* and *was given*, for example.

In all of the above sentences, the subject does not do the action in the verb; rather, the subject receives the action in the verb. If we made the subject the doer of the action in the verb, we woud write the sentences differently. Compare the following lists:

Subject Does the Action	Subject Receives the Action
a. The waiter <u>served</u> the meals.	The meals *are served*.
b. Someone <u>gave</u> an award to the restaurant.	The award *was given*.
c. The award <u>thrilled</u> the chef.	The chef *was thrilled*.
d. Her secretarial job <u>bored</u> Laura.	Laura *got bored*.
e. A restaurant <u>hired</u> Laura.	Laura *was hired*.
f. The new boss <u>pays</u> her well.	Laura *gets paid* well.

When the subject receives the action in the verb, we use a form of the helping verb *be* or *get* followed by the past participle.

Exercise 5

First underline any forms of *have*, *be* or *get*, and make sure that the main verbs following them have *-ed* endings or irregular past participle endings.

incorrect: I <u>was</u> hire by the phone company, but I <u>haven't</u> begin the job jet.

correct: I was **hired** by the phone company, but I haven't **begun** the job yet.

---

1. I always get bore during the lectures in my economics class.

2. A whole family of mice has occupy my kitchen.

3. Many adults are prejudice against the music their children listen to.

4. The city's plan to build a new baseball stadium has backfire.

5. Rock singers are often stereotype as stupid and rebellious.

6. In my role as a student, I try to be well-prepare for classes, quizzes and tests.

7. In his new apartment, Jim won't be disturb by the neighbors because the ceilings have been soundproof.

8. Carla has took many books out of the library, but she hasn't return any of them.

9. Sometimes I get frustrate when I try to write term papers.

10. The new stadium will be pay for with municipal bonds.

Pattern 2:   Adjectives Formed from Verbs

Some words with *-ed* endings (past participles) actually work like adjectives, and modify nouns. In the sentence

> *The chef tossed the salad,*

tossed is the verb, the word that shows the time or tense. But the same word may also be an adjective:

> We enjoyed the *tossed* salad at dinner last night.

In the above sentence, *tossed* is no longer a verb because it doesn't show time or tense in the sentence. *Tossed* modifies or describes the noun *salad*, so it is an adjective.

Adjectives formed from verbs may come before the nouns they modify:

> The *assigned* homework was difficult.

Or they may come after the nouns they modify:

> The homework *assigned by the teacher* was very difficult.

Whether they come before or after the noun, these adjectives formed from verbs normally keep their *-ed* or irregular past participle endings.

Look over this list of commonly-used adjectives formed from verbs; you'll recognize many of them. Notice that all of the adjectives come from past tense verbs or past participles.

scared children	*frozen* yogurt	*complicated* problems
frightened children	*ground* coffee beans	densely-*populated* cities
terrified children	*fried* bananas	*polluted* rivers
bored students	*baked* apples	*congested* freeways
determined students	*canned* peas	*stalled* cars
tired students	*medicated* cough drops	

motivated workers	*used* books
informed voters	*torn* magazines
prejudiced people	*polished* furniture
well-known politicians	*broken* glass
concerned citizens	*framed* pictures
confused patient	
satisfied customers	*unidentified* flying object

Exercise 6

In the following exercise, make the verb in the first sentence into an adjective modifying a noun in the second sentence.

Example: The class bored the students.

The <u>bored</u> students fell asleep.

---

1. A tornado recently damaged many homes.

   The _____ homes were costly to repair.

2. Some people abandoned their homes.

   The _____ homes were often uninhabitable.

3. The tornado terrified people living in its path.

   The _____ people went into their storm cellars.

4. The news of the tornado shocked my cousin.

   My _____ cousin had never experienced a tornado before.

5. The tornado frightened the children.

   The _____ children stayed close to their parents.

6. The work of repairing the homes exhausted the workmen.

   The _____ workmen sat down to rest.

7. Finally, the workers repaired the houses.

   The _____ houses looked like homes again.

8. But the possibility of another tornado still concerned the homeowners.

   The _____ homeowners purchased tornado insurance.

Exercise 7

Find all of the words in the following sentences which need -*ed* endings (or irregular past participle endings) and fill in the missing letters. Look especially for verb forms following *be*, *have* or *get*, and for -*ed* ending adjectives formed from verbs.

incorrect: The students were concern because no one came to the schedule meeting.

correct: The students were **concerned** because no one came to the **scheduled** meeting.

---

1.   Many of the sale items were purchase quickly by the numerous customers.

2.   Student fees were raise this semester, and many irritate students have protest

        to the administration.

3.   The room was examine for clues, but the frighten witnesses refused to help the

        detective in his efforts to solve the crime.

4.   Twenty-five points were score by the visiting team by the second quarter, and the

        frustrate fans of the home team knew that they wouldn't win.

5.   The SPCA has express concern about the large number of abandon pets, and

        they have claimed that the number of pets who are abuse by their owners is

        on the rise as well.

6.   The flight was delay because of poor weather conditions, but after a few hours,

        the plane took off.

7.   The tests have to be score by hand, so the teacher is upset because he wants

        them to be return tomorrow.

8.   The firemen were concern because the abandon building was a fire hazard.

Sometimes writers who are trying to use *-ed* endings correctly use them when they shouldn't. In the two patterns that follow, <u>the verb form never takes an *-ed* ending</u>:

1.   If the verb follows the word *to*.

incorrect:	We wanted *to crowned* him king.
correct:	We wanted *to crown* him king.

2.   If the verb form immediately follows one of the modals, or helping verbs, below:

can	*may*	*must*
could	*might*	*do/does/did*
will	*shall*	
would	*should*	

incorrect:	*Did* he *studied* for the test?
correct:	*Did* he *study* for the test?

incorrect:	We *can walked* to the movie theater.
correct:	We *can walk* to the movie theater.

LOUIE'S & THE CLIFF HOUSE
AT SEAL ROCK

Exercise 8

Proofread the following passage for correct use -d or -ed endings or irregular past participle endings. Some words should <u>not</u> have -ed endings.

Last week Tom and his wife witness a horrible robbery. As they were walking along the street one evening, they pass a dark alley. When Tom pause to glanced into the alleyway, he notice that a man had been push up against a wall of a building. Another man stood in front of him holding a load gun. Tom watch as the terrify victim hand over his wallet filled with credit cards, pieces of identification, and some cash. Tom's wife turn to see what he was looking at, and she suddenly scream. The robber turn, quickly stuff the wallet into the pocket of his coat, then fire at them with the gun, but fortunately miss them. The frighten couple ran to help the robbery victim. The man was scare; still, they were glad to discover that he was basically unharm. A reward has been offer for the capture of the robber. Tom and his wife were ask by the police to give as much information as they could remembered, but since it had been so dark, their description was fill was contradictions. No one could identified the robber, so the police haven't caught him yet.

Proofreading Tips

Always begin proofreading by reading your work out loud, reading exactly what you have written. Often we can catch missing or incorrectly-used *-ed* endings when we hear the error. Then follow this process:

1. If you have a problem with *-ed* endings on regular or irregular verbs, try following these steps:

    (a) To see if you have used simple past tense *-ed* endings correctly, go through your essay and underline any verbs. Ask yourself what time period you want to refer to. If the time is in the past, the verb should have an *-ed* ending or irregular past ending.

    (b) Now look at any forms of *have* (*has*, *have*, *had*, *having*), *be* (*am*, *is*, *are*, *was*, *were*, *be*, *been*, *being*) and *get* (*get*, *got*).
    Are any of them followed by another verb form?
    If so, does the main verb--the verb form that comes after *have*, *be*, or *get*--need an *-ed* or irregular past participle ending?

2. To catch missing *-ed* endings on adjectives formed from verbs, look at each word describing, or modifying, a noun.
    Can the adjective be made into a verb?
    Can the noun receive the action in the verb?
    If the answer to both questions is "yes," almost always the adjective should have an *-ed* ending.

3. Finally, check to make sure that you haven't added an *-ed* ending to a verb form that should not have an *-ed* ending: verb forms after *to*, and verb forms after the modals (*do, does, did, can, could, will, would, should, may, might, must* and *shall*).

7. Special Tenses: Present Perfect and Past Perfect

Present Perfect (Past-to-Present)

We have two basic reasons for using the present perfect (past-to-present):

1) <u>to show that a situation began in the past and still continues into the present</u>

> Carl <u>has lived</u> in Texas *for many years*.　　(He still lives there.)

> Carl and Jim <u>have lived</u> in Texas *since 1985*.　　(They still live there.)

If we want to show the continuous nature of a situation, we use another form:

> Carl <u>has been living</u> in Texas *since 1985*.

Whenever you use *since* to name a specific time in the past (*since 1985, since I was a child, since yesterday*), you have to use present perfect.

Use the simple past if a situation no longer exists:

> Carl <u>lived</u> in Utah before moving to Texas.　　(He no longer lives in Utah.)

2) <u>to show a situation that happened at an unspecified time in the past</u>

> She <u>has visited</u> Mexico.　　(We don't know exactly when.)

> I <u>have seen</u> that movie several times.　　(We don't know exactly when.)

In both sentences, the experience, rather than the specific time or number of events, is emphasized.

Use simple past tense if a specific past point in time is mentioned:

> She <u>visited</u> Mexico *last summer*.

> I <u>saw</u> that movie again *yesterday*.

We have three forms of the present perfect:

1)   *has/have + -ed* ending (past participle):

My family <u>has lived</u> in San Francisco for many years.

My cousins <u>have lived</u> in San Francisco since 1992.

2)   *has/have + been + -ing* word (present participle):

My family <u>has been living</u> in San Francisco for as long as I can remember.

I <u>have been studying</u> Spanish since I was in middle school.

3)   *has/have + been + -ed* ending (past participle):

They <u>have been cheated</u> by their landlord many times.

She <u>has been fired</u> twice.

Exercise 1

Examine the sentences presented in the previous section on the two reasons for using the present perfect, and decide, in each sentence below, why the present perfect was used.

Mark 1 if it shows a situation that began in the past and continues into the present:

    __1__   My boss <u>has worked</u> at the Magic Spa for two years.

Mark 2 if it indicates that something happened at an unspecified time in the past:

    __2__   Cheryl <u>has starred</u> in a TV commercial.

_____   1.   Frank has made several videos of his family vacations.

_____   2.   My brothers have liked science-fiction movies since they were children.

_____   3.   I have already seen that movie.

_____   4.   Their store has been burglarized many times.

_____   5.   I have tried to reach you by phone for hours.

_____   6.   A new vaccine has been developed.

_____   7.   Professor Carlson has been teaching at this university for two years.

_____   8.   No one has seen Mark since Tuesday.

_____   9.   I have been working on my essay for five hours.

_____   10.   The bay has always been polluted.

Exercise 2

Use either the present perfect or the simple past as needed.

Examples: I (visit) <u>visited</u> my sister *last night.*

I (visit) <u>have visited</u> my sister *many times this week.*

___

1.   I (go) _____ to a movie with Amy last night.

2.   I (see) _____ many movies with Amy since we met.

3.   Frank (play) _____ baseball since he was a little boy.

4.   Bill (be) _____ in Chicago for two weeks.

5.   I (read) _____ many books since summer began.

Last week, I (read) _____ three historical novels.

6.   For several years, medical researchers around the world (do) _____

a great deal of research on AIDS.

7.   Families (change) _____ a great deal in this century.

8.   Yesterday in my psychology class, I (learn) _____ why some people

are afraid of being in a small crowded space.

9.   I (know) _____ Diana for several years, but I just recently

(discover) _____ that she has a twin sister.

10.   Cindy (borrow) _____ several books last month and

still (return, not) _____ them.

Exercise 3

This paragraph discusses the writer's experiences as a language learner. The moment of speaking or writing is now, so some of the verbs are in the present tense. Many of the verbs are in the simple past tense, but some of them should be in the present perfect (past-to-present). Change the verbs that are inappropriate in the simple past tense to present perfect. (Do not change present tense verbs.)

I think that I should speak at least three languages. I can speak English, my native language, and I studied Spanish all my life, so I can speak two languages fluently. For many years, I wanted to learn how to speak Portuguese, and now I finally have the opportunity because I enrolled in a beginning Portuguese class last month. Since then, I went to class regularly and studied the assigned textbook, but my pronunciation is comical, so I work with a tutor every Tuesday. Luckily, my tutor also speaks Spanish and traveled many times in Spain, Portugal, and South America, so he can answer my questions about language and culture. He helped me a great deal, especially with idioms, which take a long time to learn, particularly if you didn't go to the country where the idioms are spoken.

PAST PERFECT (Past-Before-Past)

We use the past perfect to show that something happened in the past before another past action:

By the time you <u>arrived</u>, I <u>had left</u>.
                 2   1

The thief simply <u>walked</u> in because I <u>had forgotten</u> to lock the door.
               2   1

Her eyes <u>were</u> red because she <u>had been crying</u>.
      2   1

In the above sentences, the past perfect (1) shows which past action happened first, and simple past tense (2) shows what happened after the first action.

But some sentences can be tricky:

Until yesterday, I <u>had</u> never <u>heard</u> about it.

In this sentence, something is missing, but understood:

What happened yesterday? *I heard about it.*
What happened before yesterday? *I didn't hear about it.*
Heard is the 2nd past action (the most recent) while *didn't hear* is the first past action, so it should be in the past perfect.

When we write about an incident that happened in the past, often two past actions happen at the same time, so be careful to use the past perfect only when necessary. In the following paragraph, all of the verbs are underlined.

As I <u>walked</u> down the lonely street at midnight, I <u>thought</u>
I <u>heard</u> footsteps behind me. The footsteps <u>grew</u> louder and louder.
I suddenly <u>stopped</u> and <u>whirled</u> around to face whoever <u>was following</u>
me. But no one <u>was</u> there. My imagination <u>had been playing</u> tricks
on me.

Only the verb in the final sentence is in the past perfect because only in this sentence does the writer refer to something (his imagination playing tricks on him) that happened at an earlier point in the story (before he turned around and discovered that no one was there).

Important: Often we don't need to use the past perfect because we make the time relationship between actions or events clear by using the time word *before* or *after*.

<table>
<tr><td>I <u>left</u> before you <u>arrived</u>.
1   2</td><td>*Before* makes it clear that the action *left* happened first.</td></tr>
<tr><td>You <u>arrived</u> after I <u>left</u>.
2   1</td><td>*After* makes it clear that the action *arrived* happened second.</td></tr>
</table>

Exercise 4

In the following sentences, use past perfect or simple past tense of the verbs given in parentheses. Read each sentence carefully before you choose the verb; remember that if the time word *before* or *after* makes the time relationship clear, you do not have to use past perfect.

> Example: Class already (start) _____by the time I arrived.
>
> Class already <u>had started</u> by the time I arrived.

---

1.   Molly (be) _____ a teacher before she (become) _____

a lawyer.

2.   Yesterday I (see) _____ Susan Chan, an old friend whom I

(see, not) _____ in many years. At first, I (recognize, not)

_____ her because she (gain) _____ fifty pounds.

3.   Joe suddenly (realize) _____ that the teacher (ask) _____

him a question.

4.   It (be) _____ midnight when I finally (go) _____ to bed.

5.   I (feel) _____ better after I (take) _____ some medicine.

6. When I (go) _____ to see my math teacher about why I (receive) _____ a failing grade on the last test, he (examine) _____ my paper and then (announce) _____ that he (make) _____ a mistake and (change) _____ my grade to an "A."

7. When I (try) _____ to explain to my friend why I (call, not) _____ him in several weeks, he (tell) _____ me not to worry because he (be) _____ out of town for a month.

8. When Sharon and Will (get married) _____ last month, they (knew) _____ each other for only two weeks.

9. I (go) _____ to the movies after I (finish) _____ my homework even though I (see) _____ the movie many times.

10. Jerry (come) _____ to the party, but no one (invite) _____ him.

Exercise 5

Much of the following paragraph is written in the simple past tense. But many of the verbs would be more appropriate in the past perfect. Change the ones that should be changed into past perfect.

All of us can think of annoying or embarrassing experiences we have had. One in particular comes to mind when I am reminiscing about the past. It occurred on the Tuesday before Thanksgiving in 1990; I just finished doing the dishes and was ready to take the garbage out. Wrapping it securely and walking downstairs, I suddenly felt something underfoot and heard a snapping noise. A second later, my feet slipped and I found myself sitting on the stairs. It got dark early, so I couldn't see very well, but I finally spotted what I stepped on: it was a very small, hard pine cone. I was so annoyed that I threw it into the neighbor's yard. Then I picked up the garbage and put it in the trash can, limped upstairs, and examined my foot. It already got red and slightly swollen. When I went to the doctor the next day, he took an X-ray, examined it and announced that I broke my foot. When I told him what happened, he laughed out loud, then sent me to have a cast put on. I never wore a cast or used crutches in my whole life, but I learned how to get around quite efficiently. Ever since then, I have had a healthy respect for the power of the pine cone.

Exercise 6

In this exercise, you will review the verb tenses you have practiced in this unit. Choose the correct verb tense of the verb in parentheses--either present perfect, simple past, or past perfect.

Example: Last year, Louise (quit) <u>quit</u> her job because she (save) <u>had saved</u>

enough money to travel around the world. When I (see) <u>saw</u>

her last week, she (tell) <u>told</u> me that she (travel) <u>had traveled</u> to

four continents. I'm jealous because I (be) <u>have been</u> to only two!

---

1.   Interest in making English the official language of the United States

(increase) _____ lately.

2.   When the Surgeon General's report (come) _____ out warning

people of the dangers of smoking, millions of Americans (quit) _____

even though they (smoke) _____ regularly.

3.   Magazines such as *Good Housekeeping* and *Family Circle* (be) _____

popular from the time they (appear) _____ on the market.

4.   By the time I (reach) _____ my thirteenth birthday five years

ago, I (spend) _____ thousands of hours watching television.

5.   When Frank (look) _____ in the mirror, he (realize) _____

that he (gain) _____ a lot of weight.

6.   The widespread use of "crack" cocaine among teenagers (be) _____

a problem the government (solve, not) _____ yet.

CITY LIGHTS ON COLUMBUS

8. Special Helping Verbs

We often use the helping verbs, or modals--*do, did, can, could, will, would, should, may, must* and *might*. But two of these helping verbs--*would* and *could*--seem to cause problems because we use them in the wrong time, or tense.

Showing Habitual Action

Present Habitual Action

We often use simple present tense to show actions that are repeated or habitual in the present:

> Mario enjoys both sunny and cloudy days. On warm sunny days, he <u>sits</u> in the sun for awhile; then he <u>waters</u> his plants, rearranges flower pots in his patio, and <u>pulls</u> weeds, or he <u>washes</u>, <u>waxes</u>, and <u>polishes</u> his car. On cloudy days, he <u>stays</u> inside and <u>reads</u> a book.

This paragraph describes Mario's usual or customary actions in his present life. Notice that we do <u>not</u> use *would* when naming present habitual action.

Past Habitual Action

If we want to show past actions that were repeated or habitual, we can use <u>*would* + base form of a verb</u>:

> When Mario lived in Colorado, he enjoyed both sunny and cloudy days. He <u>would sit</u> in the sun for awhile; then he <u>would water</u> his plants, <u>rearrange</u> flower pots in his patio, and <u>pull</u> weeds, or he <u>would wash</u>, <u>wax</u>, and <u>polish</u> his car. On cloudy days, he <u>would stay</u> inside and <u>read</u> a book.

This paragraph describes Mario's usual or customary actions when he lived in Colorado--past actions that he performed regularly and routinely. We use <u>*would* + verb</u> to show past habitual behavior.

More often, we use both _would_ + verb forms and simple past tense verbs when we write about a past time, because some of the actions are habitual or customary, while others are states of being or feelings, or actions that aren't habitual. Read the following paragraph; each verb is underlined.

> Some years ago, my grandfather <u>died</u>, but my memories of him are vivid to this day. He <u>enjoyed</u> being around small children, and <u>would sing</u> to them, rocking them back and forth in an old overstuffed rocking chair. He <u>would invent</u> silly games, which they <u>loved</u>, and <u>would come up with</u> even sillier jokes, making everyone under the age of six laugh. He <u>would help</u> anyone in need, and since he <u>was married</u> to a woman who <u>had</u> seven sisters, there <u>was</u> always someone, somewhere, in need of help. But he never <u>wanted</u> the rest of the family to know about his generosity; he <u>liked</u> his acts of kindness to be secrets.

The above paragraph has two kinds of verbs:

1	2
died	_would_ sing
enjoyed	_would_ invent
loved	_would_ come up with
was married	_would_ help
had	
was	
wanted	
liked	

The verbs in the first list name states of being or of feeling; the verbs in the second name acts or events. We use _would_ with the second group to show that the actions named took place on a regular, habitual, or customary basis:

He. . .<u>would</u> always <u>sing.</u>   (He regularly sang to them.)

He <u>would invent</u> silly games.   (He had the habit of inventing silly games.)

He <u>would</u> always <u>help</u> anyone.   (He had a custom of helping people.)

As a general rule, when you want to show regular, habitual past actions, you can use _would_ + base form of the verb. The verb should be the kind shown in the second list-- verbs that name actions or events rather than states of being or conditions of life.

Exercise 1

Write a paragraph in which you describe the routine you follow <u>now,</u> after you get home from school. Use the present tense to name any habitual or customary actions or events.

After I get home from school, _____

_____

_____

_____

_____

_____

_____

Exercise 2

Now write a paragraph describing the routine you followed after school <u>when you were an elementary school student</u>. Use *would* + base form of the verb to describe customary actions, and simple past tense verbs to name states of being or feeling.

After I got home from elementary school, _____

_____

_____

_____

_____

_____

_____

Showing Ability

Writers often confuse the helping verbs *can* and *could* when writing about abilities.

Use *can* to show present ability.

To show present ability, use <u>can + base form of the verb</u>. If we know how to do something now, we can say:

I *can swim.*	=	I *know how to swim.*
Sam *can speak* Tagalog.	=	Sam *knows how to speak* Tagalog.

Use *could* to show past ability.

To show past ability, use <u>could + base form of the verb</u>. If we knew how to do something in the past, we can say:

I *could swim* when I was five.	=	I *knew how to swim* when I was five.
Sam *could speak* Tagalog as a boy.	=	Sam *knew how to speak* Tagalog as a boy.

Exercise 3

Write 5 sentences naming abilities you have <u>now</u> (things you know how to do now). Use <u>can + base form of the verb</u> to show present abilities.

Example: Now that I'm a college student, I *can do* research well.

1. _____

2. _____

3. _____

4. _____

5. _____

Exercise 4

Write 5 sentences naming abilities you had (things you knew how to do) when you were a child. Use <u>could + base form of the verb</u> to show past ability.

Example: When I was ten, I *could ski* like a pro.

_____

1.   _____

2.   _____

3.   _____

4.   _____

5.   _____

Note: the verbs following *would*, *can* and *could*, and any other modals, don't have *-ed* or *-s* endings.

THE PALACE OF FINE ARTS – the Marina

Exercise 5

In the following sentences, correct any errors in verbs showing present and past habitual action or present and past ability. Check to see that simple present tense shows present habitual actions and *would* + base form of the verb shows past habitual actions. Check to see that *can* shows present ability and *could* shows past ability.

incorrect: Every day when I finish my homework, I would watch a movie.
correct: Every day when I finish my homework, I **watch** a movie.

incorrect: Now I could understand the novel that I couldn't understand yesterday.
correct: Now I **can understand** the novel that I couldn't understand yesterday.

---

1. Usually I would buy coffee when I arrive on campus so I could be more alert.

2. This semester, I review my notes and would test myself before every test.

3. When I was in high school, I can work with computers as well as any adult.

4. Michael could drive now, but he couldn't when he was in his twenties.

5. As a young child, I would visit my grandmother every Sunday, but now I couldn't because she lives too far away.

6. Men and women would usually share the housework now, but twenty years ago, men rarely would do any housework.

7. Now I usually go over to my best friend's house every Saturday night because she could make the best pasta dinners.

8. Athough Tia is only four, she could already read and would read all the time.

9. Contemporary families generally would spend less time doing family activities.

10. Now that I'm an adult, I could stay out as late as I want.

9. Conditionals

Look at the following sentence:

>   If Mary finishes her homework, she will go to the movies with you.

If we break it down, we see that this sentence begins with an "if" clause. "If" means "in case," "in the event that," "on condition that," "when," or "whenever." In other words, in an "if" sentence, we're saying that in order for something to happen, something else must happen. We state the condition in the "if" clause, and we state the event that will happen, if the condition is met, in the main clause.

IF can be used in two kinds of statements: **A) regular** and **B) hypothetical**.

A)   Regular conditionals

1.   <u>indicate events or actions that are really possible</u>:

>   If Mary finishes her homework, she'll go to the movies with you.
>   *(There's a good chance that Mary will finish her homework,
>   and then she will go to the movies.)*

<u>Verb Tense</u>:   When the regular conditional indicates events or actions that are really possible, the "if" clause states the present condition in the present tense, and the main clause states the resulting event in the future tense.

More Examples:

"If" Clause/present tense	Main Clause/future tense
If Jack <u>earns</u> enough money,	he <u>will buy</u> a car.
If I <u>find</u> a better job,	I <u>will need</u> a new wardrobe.
If the ozone layer <u>deteriorates</u>,	the climate <u>will change</u>.

2.   **Regular conditionals** <u>also express habitual or customary behavior:</u>

If Mary finishes her homework, she watches television.
> *(Mary has a regular routine; whenever she finishes her homework, she almost always watches television.)*

<u>Verb Tense</u>: When the conditional sentence expresses present habitual behavior, we use present tense verbs in <u>both</u> the "if" clause and the main clause.

More Examples:

"If" Clause/present tense	**Main Clause/present tense**
If the Giants <u>lose</u>,	Larry <u>cries</u>.
If I <u>eat</u> too much chocolate,	I <u>get</u> sick.
If Joe <u>drives</u> on a sunny day,	he <u>wears</u> prescription sunglasses.

In the above three sentences expressing habitual behavior, notice that "whenever" can be used instead of "if."

Just Desserts — Irving

Exercise 1

Think of a main clause to add to each of the "if" clauses, and then write it in the space provided. Be sure to use future tense to indicate an action that will happen in the future if the condition is met, and present tense to indicate a customary or habitual action.

Example: If Pete moves in with Martha, _____

           If Pete moves in with Martha, *he will have to adjust to her loud singing.*

Example: If (whenever) Pete lives with anyone, _____

           If (whenever) Pete lives with anyone, *he does his share of the housework.*

1.   If Pete gets his own apartment, _____

_____

2.   If he decides to get a roommate, _____

_____

3.   If he decides to live alone, _____

_____

4.   If he doesn't do his laundry, _____

_____

5.   If he doesn't pay his rent on time, _____

_____

6.   If his landlord raises his rent, _____

_____

Past Regular Conditionals

If we use the past tense in the "if" clause in regular conditionals, we mean that if something happened in the past, we can infer that something else probably is happening, already happened, or will happen; we express our inference in the main clause.

We can express an inference about the <u>present effect</u> of a past tense condition by using present tense in the main clause:

Past Condition   **Inference about the Present**

If Mary <u>went</u> to the movies,   she <u>is</u> probably home now.
(We don't know if Mary went to the movies, but if she did, we infer that she is home now.)

If Pete <u>moved</u> in with Martha,   he <u>is paying</u> half of the rent.
(We don't know if Pete moved in with Martha, but if he did, we infer that they are sharing the rent.)

We can also express an inference about the <u>past effect</u> of a past condition by using past tense in the main clause:

Past Condition   **Inference about the Past**

If Mary <u>went</u> to the movies,   she probably <u>saw</u> a horror film.
(We don't know if Mary went to the movies, but if she did, we guess that she saw a horror film.)

If Pete <u>moved</u> in with Martha,   he <u>adjusted</u> to her loud singing.
(We don't know if he moved in with Martha, but if he did, he probably got used to her singing.)

Or we can express an inference about a possible <u>future effect</u> of a past condition by using future tense in the main clause:

Past Condition   **Inference about the Future**

If Mary <u>went</u> to the movies,   she <u>will tell</u> us the whole plot.
(We don't know if she went, but if she did, we assume she'll tell us the plot.)

If Pete <u>moved</u> in with Martha,   he <u>will adjust</u> to her loud singing.
(We don't know if Pete moved in, but we assume he will adjust to her singing.)

Exercise 2

The verb tenses in the "if" clauses from Exercise 1 have been changed to past tense. Write three main clauses for each "if" clause, expressing inferences about the effects of a past condition, using first present tense, then past tense, and then future tense.

Example: If Pete <u>moved</u> in with Martha, *he is very happy*.
                                                present tense

             If Pete <u>moved</u> in with Martha, *he made friends with her cats*.
                                                past tense

             If Pete <u>moved</u> in with Martha, *he probably will move out soon*.
                                                future tense

_____

1.   If Pete got his own apartment, _____
                                                present tense

        If Pete got his own apartment, _____
                                                past tense

        If Pete got his own apartment, _____
                                                future tense

2.   If he decided to get a roommate, _____
                                                present tense

        If he decided to get a roommate, _____
                                                past tense

        If he decided to get a roommate, _____
                                                future tense

3.   If he decided to live alone, _____
                                                present tense

        If he decided to live alone, _____
                                                past tense

        If he decided to live alone, _____
                                                future tense

94

4.   If he didn't do his laundry, _____
                                          present tense

      If he didn't do his laundry, _____
                                          past tense

      If he didn't do his laundry, _____
                                          future tense

5.   If he didn't pay his rent on time, _____
                                          present tense

      If he didn't pay his rent on time, _____
                                          past tense

      If he didn't pay his rent on time, _____
                                          future tense

6.   If his landlord raised his rent, _____
                                          present tense

      If his landlord raised his rent, _____
                                          past tense

      If his landlord raised his rent, _____
                                          future tense

B.   Hypothetical Conditionals

Read the following paragraph:

> Jeff lives in San Francisco. If the weather is warm, he
>
> swims in the Bay. But if he lived in Hawaii, he would swim in
>
> the ocean all year.

What is the one known fact stated in this paragraph? _____

The second and third sentences in the paragraph both contain "if" clauses, but even though they look alike, they aren't. The first one is just like the ones you've already worked on; it names something that's really possible: *the weather might get warm.* The second "if" clause, though, is contrary to the given fact: *Jeff doesn't live in Hawaii, but in San Francisco.*

We use hypothetical "if" clauses to express something that is contrary to fact; the conditional states an improbable or unreal condition. We show that a condition is hypothetical by using a past tense form of the verb in the "if" clause.

In present hypothetical conditionals, we use the past tense in the "if" clause and *would* or *could* plus base form of the verb in the main clause:

"IF" Clause Past Tense	Main Clause *would* or *could* + base form of the verb
If Jeff <u>had</u> a million dollars,	he <u>would travel</u> around the world.
If Jeff <u>lived</u> in Hawaii,	he <u>could surf</u> Waimea Bay.
or: If Jeff <u>could live</u> in Hawaii,	he <u>could surf</u> Waimea Bay.

NOTE: When we form hypothetical conditionals using the verb *BE*, we use the verb *WERE*, no matter what the subject is:

If I <u>were</u> a millionaire,   I would buy my own jct.
If Mary <u>were</u> a millionaire, she would donate her money to charity.
If we <u>were</u> millionaires,   my husband and I would retire.

Exercise 3

Following are beginnings of present hypothetical conditionals. The "if" clauses are correctly written in the past tense. Complete the sentences by adding a main clause to each, choosing the correct verb form: *would* or *could* + base form of a verb.

Example: If Joe had a day off from school, *he would go to the beach*.

If Joe had a day off from school, *he could sleep all day*.

1.   If I had a lot of money, _____

2.   If I did not have to go to work, _____

3.   If the book were not full of technical terms, _____

4.   If we were more physically fit, _____

5.   If Christmas came in July, _____

6.   If the population of my neighborhood doubled overnight, _____

_____

7.   If I were older, _____

8.   If our classes were smaller, _____

Read the following paragraph:

> (1) I realize that a program of regular exercise would bring me a number of benefits. (2) I would improve my cardio-vascular system, (3) which can probably stand improving, (4) and I would probably get rid of some of the fat around my waist. (5) That would be a definite benefit (6) because I am beginning to need new clothes that fit. (7) All in all, I would certainly benefit by beginning an aerobics class or jogging three or four times a week.

Now go back and circle all verbs with *would* or *could*.

The conditional verbs in clauses 1, 2, 4, 5, and 7 are all based on an unstated "if" idea or condition: *if I were to begin a program of regular exercise. . . .*

Sometimes we write paragraphs like this one, in which the "if" idea is not stated directly, but is implied. In these paragraphs, not every verb needs to have a conditional form. For instance, the verbs in clauses 3 and 6 name situations that are actually true, so the verbs are not in conditional forms.

To avoid confusing a reader about what's real or factual and what's hypothetical, we have to choose the correct verb forms.

Exercise 4

The following passage presents a hypothetical situation along with factual material. Fill in the blanks with conditionals using *would* or *could* or with factual verb forms as appropriate.

If San Francisco had a major earthquake, the city would suffer major damage.

The earthquake (destroy) _____ almost all of the older large buildings,

and (damage) _____ even many of the new ones in the downtown

area, for their designs (not, test) _____ in an actual major earthquake

elsewhere. Gas, electricity, and phone service (stop) _____ for weeks in

many areas, and families throughout the city (not, be) _____ able to

cook meals or heat their houses. Many of these houses (collapse) _____

because they (not, bolt) _____ to their foundations. Essential

businesses such as food stores (close) _____ for indefinite periods,

and looting and other forms of lawlessness (occur) _____ because

police services (be) _____overextended. A catastrophic fire such

as the one that (happen) _____ during the 1906 earthquake

(be) _____ a real danger because water mains (break) _____

throughout the city. In short, although most people (find) _____ life

in San Francisco as pleasant and rewarding as it is anywhere in the world, a major

earthquake (make) _____ life difficult at best.

Past Hypothetical Conditionals

We use past hypothetical conditionals to express past hypothetical conditions that would have caused a different outcome--in the past or in the present.

If we want to show how a past hypothetical condition would affect <u>the present</u>, we use past perfect (past before past) in the "if" clause and *would* or *could* + main verb in the main clause.

Past Hypothetical Condition	**Present Effect**
If I <u>had made</u> more money last year, *(I didn't make more money.)*	I <u>could go</u> on a trip this year.
If I <u>had been</u> more talented as a child, *(I wasn't talented enough.)*	I <u>would be</u> a concert pianist now.
If Mario <u>had known</u> what dentistry was like, *(He didn't know what dentistry was like.)*	he <u>wouldn't be</u> a dentist now.

If we want to show how a past hypothetical condition would have affected <u>the past</u>, we use past perfect (past-before-past) in the "if" clause and *would have* or *could have* + the past participle in the main clause.

Past Hypothetical Condition	**Past Effect**
If I <u>had made</u> more money last year,	I <u>would have gone</u> on a vacation. *(I didn't go on vacation.)*
If I <u>had been</u> more talented as a child,	I <u>could have been</u> a concert pianist. *(I'm not a concert pianist.)*
If Mario <u>had known</u> what dentistry was like,	he never <u>would have become</u> a dentist. *(He is a dentist, but wishes he weren't.)*

Exercise 5

Following are past time hypothetical "if" clauses. Complete the sentences by adding first a main clause showing a present effect, and then a main clause showing a past effect. Be sure you select the appropriate verb form to show either a hypothetical present effect or a hypothetical past effect.

Example: If I had stayed in graduate school, <u>I would be a social worker now</u>.
present effect

or: If I had stayed in graduate school, <u>I would have gotten my masters</u>.
past effect

_____

1.   If Frank had quit his job last year, _____
present effect

If Frank had quit his job last year, _____
past effect

2.   If my parents had not met, _____
present effect

If my parents had not met, _____
past effect

3.   If we had bought a better car, _____
present effect

If we had bought a better car, _____
past effect

4.   If I had not graduated from high school, _____
present effect

If I had not graduated from high school, _____
past effect

5.   If our team had won the World Series, _____
present effect

If our team had won the World Series, _____
past effect

Exercise 6

The following passage presents a past hypothetical situation along with factual material. Fill in the blanks with the correct forms of the verbs provided, making sure to use conditional or factual verb forms as appropriate.

To show a <u>present effect</u> of a past hypothetical situation, use *would* or *could* + a main verb in the main clause:

If our team had won the game, we <u>could be</u> in the playoffs.

To show a <u>past effect</u> of a past hypothetical situation, use *would have* or *could have* + the past participle in the main clause:

If our team had won the game, I <u>would have treated</u> everyone to dinner.

If the South had won the American Civil War, history would have taken a different shape. The South (extend) _____ its control over the areas that are now New Mexico, Arizona, Oklahoma, and possibly even Baja California, and a second war with Mexico possibly (happen) _____. Although modern historians (agree) _____ that slavery (be) _____ a dying institution even in the mid-19th century, it certainly (continue) _____ much longer than it did. It (be) _____ interesting to speculate on whether two separate relatively weak American nations (survive) _____ into the 20th century or whether the inherently stronger North gradually (absorb) _____ the Southern states back into a national union or (reconquer) _____ the South by force of arms.

10. Pronoun Agreement

We replace specific nouns with pronouns to avoid repetition. Without pronouns, some of our sentences might look like this:

> When Sara had lunch with Roger, Roger told Sara about Roger's geology class and where Roger's geology class was going on Roger's geology class' field trip.

Using pronouns, we make the sentence less wordy but maintain its clarity:

> When Sara had lunch with Roger <u>he</u> told <u>her</u> about <u>his</u> geology class and where <u>it</u> was going on <u>its</u> field trip.

Sometimes when we use a pronoun, we forget to look back and see if the noun that we are referring to is singular or plural. As a subject must agree with its verb, a pronoun must agree in number with the noun it refers to.

Exercise 1

Change the following sentences so that the pronouns agree.

> **Example:** Last week, I forgot to water my plants, so it wilted.
> **Correct:** Last week, I forgot to water my plants, so **they** wilted.

The pronoun *it* refers to *plants*, but since *plants* is plural, the pronoun needs to be *they*.

---

1. Many people have 9 to 5 jobs and work very hard at it.

2. I enjoy playing many sports, but I also like watching it on television.

3. My cats are happy when my neighbor feeds it leftovers.

4. Each of my sisters has their own car.

5. My problems with my boss started off small, but later it evolved into something bigger.

Pronouns: a special problem

English does not have a gender-free singular pronoun referring to people, so writers used to write sentences like this one:

> When a photographer shoots, <u>he</u> must try to make <u>his</u> subject appear natural.

But now many people feel that the automatic use of <u>he</u> excludes women, that the sentence above, for example, might suggest that all photographers are male. So now we use other options to make our pronouns agree. We can include both sexes:

> When a photographer shoots, <u>he or she</u> must try to make <u>his or her</u> subject appear natural.

But many readers also find this method wordy. One other option, when it makes sense in the context of our writing, is to make the pronoun and the noun it refers to plural:

> When photographers shoot, they must try to make their subjects appear natural.

Exercise Two

Correct the following pronoun errors.

> Example: When a person takes too many classes, they fall behind in their assignments.

Since *a person* is singular, but *they* is plural, the pronoun does not agree with the noun it refers to. To fix this, try either one of these choices:

Correct (option one): When **a person** takes too many classes, **he or she** often falls behind in **his or her** assignments.
Correct (option two): When **people** take too many classes, **they** often fall behind in **their** assignments.

---

1. If a person is going to commit crimes, they should be prepared to face the consequences.

2. Even though the average student tries to use their time wisely, they often fall prey to the many distractions of college life.

3. Someone called late last night, but they hung up when I answered the phone.

4. When a person goes to the supermarket, they should bring a list.

Shift in Person

Pronouns can be divided into three groups:

1)   The <u>first person</u>:   I/me   we/us

2)   The <u>second person</u>:   you

3)   The <u>third person</u>:   she/her he/him one they/them

Problems occur when you switch from one group to the other group mid-sentence:

incorrect: When <u>one</u> is tired and under stress, <u>you</u> can have difficulty concentrating.

Since *one* and *you* don't refer to the same "person," the reader of the sentence can become confused about who it is the writer is referring to.
The sentence can be corrected in any of the following ways:

When <u>you</u> are tired and under stress, <u>you</u> can have difficulty concentrating.

When <u>one</u> is tired and under stress, <u>she or he</u> can have difficulty concentrating.

When <u>people</u> are tired and under stress, <u>they</u> can have difficulty concentrating.

Exercise 3

Correct the following sentences so that pronouns agree. See the sentences above for possible solutions.

---

1.   When one is very young, you often don't understand the pressures that parents face.

2.   I liked the movie because it kept you on the edge of your seat.

3.   Professor Clark told us that we don't have to answer the last essay question unless you want to skip one of the first four.

4.   Either one can seek learning experiences or they can live for their possessions.

5.   When you go shopping, one should have a specific list.

11. Possessive Nouns

The possessive forms of nouns show possession, or ownership. We can show possession without changing the noun itself:

> the dog belonging to the *boy*

> the talent of the *singer*

But a simpler, more common way is to change the noun that does the possessing:

> the *boy's* dog

> the *singer's* talent

With a few exceptions, the following two rules cover nearly all you need to know about forming possessives:

1. <u>To form the possessive of a noun, add apostrophe + *s*</u>:

   the books of the *student*   =   the *student's* books

   the toys of the *girl*   =   the *girl's* toys

2. <u>If the noun already ends in *s*, just add an apostrophe</u>:

   the books of the *students* =   the *students'* books

   the toys of the *girls*   =   the *girls'* toys

If a proper noun (a name) ends in *s*, you may choose to add either apostrophe + *s*, or just the apostrophe alone, depending on whether you would pronounce the extra *s*.
For instance:

> *Moses'* followers   OR   *Moses's* followers

Reminder: Do not use *'s* when you are just showing plural form:

> correct: Charbroiled hot dogs are served here.

> incorrect: Charbroiled hot dog's are served here.

Exercise 1

Rewrite each underlined group of words, using apostrophes to show possession.

Examples: He liked the looks of the car.

the car's looks

He remembered the names of all of the dogs.

all of the dogs' names

---

1.   I liked <u>the features of the car</u>.

2.   I liked <u>the features of the cars</u>.

3.   We admired <u>the stars of the show</u>.

4.   We admired <u>the stars of the shows</u>.

5.   John was surprised at <u>the skill of the players</u>.

6.   He was not surprised at <u>the record of the team</u>.

7.   The new governor was not <u>the choice of the people</u>.

8.   They liked <u>the clothing of the store</u>.

9.   Sheila feeds <u>the pets of her neighbors</u>.

10.   I unexpectedly ran into <u>the daughter of my boss</u>.

11.   James edited <u>the essay of Carlos</u>.

12.   He agrees with <u>the foreign policies of the government</u>.

Other Forms of Possessives

Here are some guidelines for other types of possessives that you will encounter from time to time.

Joint Possession: The following pairs of nouns show joint ownership; two or more people own the same thing.

the duck belonging to *Sid and Eddie* = *Sid and Eddie's* duck

the children of *Tina and Al* = *Tina and Al's* children

Rule: Nouns showing joint ownership have apostrophe + *s* added to the noun nearest to the thing possessed.

Individual Possession: The following pairs of nouns show individual ownership. (Sid and Eddie probably do not own the same shoes, nor do Tina and Al use the same toothbrush.)

the shoes belonging to *Sid and Eddie* = *Sid's and Eddie's* shoes

the toothbrushes of *Tina and Al* = *Tina's and Al's* toothbrushes

Rule: Nouns showing individual ownership have apostrophe + *s* added to each noun.

When NOT to use 'S:

Do not use 's to form possessive pronouns;

Pronouns	Possessive Pronouns
he	his
she	her/hers
it	its
we	our/ours
you	your/yours
they	their/theirs
I	my/mine

What possessive pronouns belong in the following examples?

This is Doris' book.
This is her book.   This book is _____.

These are Fred's and Ted's bikes.
These are their bikes.   These bikes are _____.

Exercise 2

Rewrite each underlined group of words, using apostrophes to show possession.

Examples: The flavor of the coffee was unusual.   *the coffee's flavor*

                   I live in the home of my parents.   *my parents' home*

                   We went to the wedding of Joe and Kay.   *Joe and Kay's wedding*

                   She ironed the clothes of Pete and May.   *Pete's and May's clothes*

---

1. The combined losses of the North and South were the greatest in any American war.

2. The president took away some of the responsibilities of the chief-of-staff.

3. We loved the shoes of George and Sara.

4. She was insulted by the rude remarks of her sister-in-law.

5. I couldn't stand the behavior of George and Sara.

6. The information of the ambassador was mostly incorrect.

7. The voyages of Magellan and Columbus were controversial.

8. The novels of Hemingway and Faulkner are among the most admired in modern literature.

9. One of the most famous events in American history is the journey west of Lewis and Clark.

10. Don't forget the birthday of your mother-in-law.

Exercise 3

Rewrite each underlined group of words using apostrophes to show possession.

Example: Professional wresters attract <u>the enthusiasm of their fans</u>.

their fans' enthusiasm

---

1. <u>The images of many proessional wrestlers</u> are outrageous.

2. But <u>the image of no one</u> has ever been weirder than that of George Wagner.

3. <u>The nickname of George Wagner</u> was Gorgeous George.

4. He was the most popular wrestler of the Forties and Fifties as well as <u>the biggest television attraction of Los Angeles.</u>

5. He was sometimes called "The Human Orchid," but the color of an orchid seemed drab compared to the magnificent costumes of George.

6. After leaving <u>the house of his parents</u> in Houston at age nineteen, George worked at odd jobs and wrestled <u>the other tough kids of Houston</u>.

7. He drifted to Oregon, winning <u>the light-heavyweight crown of the state</u>.

8. <u>The income of George</u> was not increasing as a result of these activities, so he decided to become a professional wrestler.

9. In this field, <u>the income of the leading wrestlers</u> is determined by their popularity.

10. <u>The turning point of the career of George</u> came when he hit upon the gimmick that no one else had tried, dressing in outrageously-colored clothes with frills and rhinestones.

Exercise 4

Proofread the sentences below. They contain both plural nouns (nouns that do not require apostrophes) and possessive nouns (nouns that do require apostrophes). When a noun is both plural and possessive, it requires an apostrophe. <u>Underline any noun ending in -s, and decide if it is possessive. If it is, add an apostrophe in the correct place.</u>

> Example: George packed his <u>clothes</u> in his <u>wifes</u> car.
>
> correct: George packed his <u>clothes</u> in his **wife's** car.

---

1. George soon began wearing the loud outfits that made him famous.

2. His managers daughter created robes for him made of fur, feathers and lace to match his wrestling trunks shocking pink color.

3. His personal valets duties included spraying Georges corner as well as his opponents face with Chanel No. 9.

4. Gorgeous Georges long, curled, bleached blond hair was his two Hungarian hairdressers handiwork.

5. His hairs true color was brown, and he always wore his hair long to imitate George Washingtons long-haired wig.

6. His imitators efforts to copy him all fell short.

7. The critics jeers failed to shake his fans affection.

8. Of course, wrestling fans affections have always been drawn to outlandish costumes and outrageous behavior.

9. Gorgeous Georges fans were no different than the fans of numerous other wrestlers who have worn bizarre costumes or taken on strange identities.

Exercise 5

Proofread the following passage for possessives, adding apostrophes where necessary to show possession.

Lake Superior is the worlds largest body of fresh water, surpassing all other inland lakes in size except the salt water Caspian Sea. Superior, like the other Great Lakes, was part of the Mississippi Rivers drainage system until Ice Age glaciers gouged deep holes in the rocks. The Glaciers handiwork shows in the shorelines rugged cliffs, (the cliffs heights reach 1500 feet) and in the ancient granite exposed there, some of the earths oldest rocks, rivaled only by those at the Grand Canyons base.

Lake Superiors first European visitor, the French explorer Brule, arrived in 1623. Of course, he didn't really discover the lake, as the Chippewa Indians had long lived on the shores of what they called Gitche Gumee. While the Indians name for the lake must have sounded strange to the Europeans, the Indians probably found the Europeans behavior stranger still, as fur traders outposts and the missions of Jesuit priests were established within decades of Brules first visit. The white mans towns and industries made the former Gitche Gumee less and less clean, until by the 1960s, the waters oxygen level was so low that fish were suffocating. But in 1972, Canada and the U. S. agreed to clean up the Great Lakes. The two nations cleanup efforts paid off in just a few years, as beaches reopened and fishermens nets again began to fill. The revival of Lake Superior demonstrated once again natures truly amazing ability to repair itself.

12. Contractions

Besides showing possession, apostrophes also show the omission of one or more letters when words are combined into **contractions**. Here is a list of some of the most common contractions.

Long Form	Contraction
I am	I'm
I had	I'd
I have	I've
it is	it's
we will	we'll
they will	they'll
we are	we're
they are	they're
do not	don't
does not	doesn't
did not	didn't
let us	let's
is not	isn't
are not	aren't
should not	shouldn't
will not	won't

Some teachers object to students using contractions in their writing and some do not. It is best to ask your teachers whether they find them acceptable or not. If you do use contractions, make sure you put the apostrophe in place of the letter or letters you omit.

THE PALACE OF THE LEGION OF HONOUR — LINCOLN PARK

Exercise 1

In each of the sentences below, correct any contraction errors you find.

Example: When John returns, he wont want to eat dinner.
Correct: When John returns, he won't want to eat dinner.

---

1.   The store is having a sale on sheets and pillowcases, but theyll probably be sold out by the end of the week.

2.   Even though theyre going to be arriving late, they will not be hungry because they will have eaten dinner on the plane.

3.   Students shouldnt wait until the night before a test to review all their class notes, for it is not the most effective way of remembering lots of detailed information.

4.   The recipes dont call for adding wine, but my mother feels that the final results arent as flavorful without it.

5.   Were planning on leaving town for the holidays, but we shouldnt be gone for more than two or three weeks.

6.   Most young people arent willing to follow their parents' advice, but they will benefit from at least listening to it.

7.   Even though good teachers dont enjoy failing students, theyre concerned about being honest with students about the quality of their work.

8.   Theyll not be arriving at the station until 8:00 p.m., so were going to have dinner at home first and then leave to pick them up.

114

Exercise 2

Proofread the sentences below for correct use of apostrophes in contractions. Make sure the apostrophe is in the proper place.

---

1. Bruno, my friend's dog, did'nt turn out to be the vicious beast Id heard about.

2. As a matter of fact, Ive never seen a dog that was more docile and well-behaved.

3. People shouldnt believe all the stories they hear about other people's pets.

4. Most dogs dont take to strangers very well to begin with, but when Bruno did'nt even bark at the sight of me, I was most surprised.

5. Bruno isnt allowed in the living room, and its amazing how he does'nt set foot within the boundaries of that particular place.

6. Bruno wont sit still, so strangers walking past the front door of my friend's home, should not approach unannounced.

7. In addition, Bruno has a curious "roommate," a cat who doesnt move outside of a self-designated area of about twelve inches in diameter.

8. Bruno and the cat didnt get into any territorial hassles when I was there, but I'd bet money that they occasionally must get into playful tiffs of one sort or another.

13. Homonyms

Homonyms are words that sound alike but do not mean the same thing and are therefore not spelled alike. These "soundalikes" are not interchangeable. If you use the wrong form in a sentence, you will confuse or mislead your reader--the last thing you want to let happen.

Your/You're

Underline all uses of *your* and *you're* in the following paragraph:

Your mother called this morning to find out if you're coming for dinner on Sunday. She wants to borrow your soufflé dish. You're going, aren't you? She also said that you're welcome to bring your friend, John, but you're going to have to watch your manners because Mrs. Moorhouse will be there, and she is not accustomed to college students and is always nervous around your friends.

    1. Which form shows ownership? _____

    2. Which is the contraction of *you + are*? _____

On the lines below, write *your* or *you're,* as appropriate.

1. _____ hot tub will be installed Monday.

2. Do you know where _____ going to put it?

3. I imagine _____ friends will want to spend the weekends at _____ now.

4. _____ going to miss _____ quiet weekends alone.

5. I realize _____ looking forward to relaxing.

6. _____ chemistry needs work if _____ going to pass the class.

7. _____ the one I want to talk to.

8. Get _____ feet off the coffee table.

Its/It's

Underline all uses of *its* and *it's* in the following paragraph:

It's surprising to many people how close the "distant past" really is to us living today. For instance, the American Civil War seems so long ago that it's almost a part of ancient history. Yet its influence lingers with us today in tensions between the North and the South; its battles are still studied by young military officers, and its last veterans died not in the dim past but in the 1950's.

Which form shows ownership? _____

Which form is the contraction of *it + is* or *it + has*? _____

On the lines below, write *its* or *it's* as appropriate.

1.   The team won _____ game with _____ chief rivals.

2.   Today _____ time to learn that "_____" is a possessive word.

3.   The rain certainly took _____ time getting here last winter.

4.   Although _____ true that _____ getting rather dark now, I think _____ still too early to go home.

5.   _____ sometimes said that France is like a miniature United States; _____ climate and geography are almost as varied as America's.

6.   _____ plain to see that the dog obeys _____ master.

7.   _____ been four years since I've been to New York.

8.   One of SFSU's disadvantages is _____ foggy weather.

9.   _____ been a long road for me; _____ taken me ten years to finish college.

Their/There/They're

Underline all uses of *their, there,* and *they're* in the following paragraph.

Mr. and Mrs. Casey are very staunch Catholics, so they're upset about their son marrying a Jewish woman. They're concernedthat their grandchildren will not have one firm religion to believe in. The Caseys know that there is some basis for their fear, since children of a religiously mixed marriage do have to cope with two religions at one time. However, they've begun to think, "So long as there is love between the parents, how can that harm the children?" In the end, they've reconciled themselves to the marriage.

1. Which form shows ownership? _____

2. Which indicates direction or is a way of introducing a thought? _____

3. Which is a contraction of *they + are*? _____

On the lines below, write *their, there,* or *they're* as appropriate.

1. _____ are three kinds of ghosts in that house.

2. _____ minds weren't on the subject the teacher was talking about.

3. _____ a lot of trouble to people who spend the night.

4. _____ is no time like the present to take care of business.

5. They tried to win _____ final game, but _____was no way they could beat _____ opponents.

6. _____ tired of doing _____ work.

7. _____ are many problems with the proposal.

8. _____ cats always get into fights.

Whose/Who's

Underline all uses of <u>whose</u> and <u>who's</u> in the following paragraph.

Who's going to the beach with us? We have to decide whose car we're going to take so we can fill it with gas. I already know who's bringing the food and drinks. Susan, whose father runs China Camp, will bring a cooler with cold drinks. Ted, who's Jeff's brother, promised to bring fried chicken and potato salad. But who's agreed to bring the napkins and eating utensils? Whose idea was this anyway?

1.   Which form shows ownership? _____
2.   Which form is the combination of
         who + is
   or   *who + has*? _____

On the lines below, write *whose* or *who's,* as appropriate.

1.   _____ picking up Sally from the airport?

2.   No one knows _____ responsible.

3.   He knows _____ fault it is.

4.   Can you find out _____ taking Kathy home?

5.   The teacher knew all along _____ idea it was to draw the picture on the board.

6.   _____ backpack is this?

7.   Jeff is the one _____ been getting A's on all the tests.

8.   We never found out _____ dog spread our garbage all over the neighborhood.

9.   Wait until you hear _____ playing at the dance Friday.

Two/To/Too

Underline all uses of *two, to,* and *too* in the following paragraph.

Strikes by employees of mass transit systems inconvenience many people. During the last Muni strike, many people had to rearrange their schedules so that they were getting to work earlier than usual and leaving later than usual. Some students found themselves in awkward situations, too, for they were unable to go to school without walking for miles. During the BART strike, too many cars cluttered the freeways and bridges, and this increase in traffic was hazardous to commuters and pedestrians alike. Just these two examples should serve to explain why I am against strikes by Muni and BART employees.

1. Which form indicates the number 2? _____
2. Which is a preposition or a part of a verb? _____
3. Which means either "also" or "very"? _____

On the lines below, write *two, to,* or *too* as appropriate.

1. It's _____ bad that many people find it _____ easy _____ settle down in front of the television rather than read a book.

2. Over-achievers try _____ hard _____ be perfect at everything they do, but they would be better off trying ___ excel at one or _____ things rather than _____ many at once.

3. My sister's _____ favorite cookie recipes call for _____ much sugar in the ingredients.

4. Pets require lots of care and attention _____ grow into healthy organisms, and plants do, _____.

5. It's _____ bad that plants aren't as stimulating ___ talk ___ as pets, though.

6. My brother is so clumsy that he finds it difficult ___ tie his shoestrings together.

7. Children who watch ___ much television usually end up with ___ crossed eyes.

More "Homonyms"

There are other "soundalikes," some of which are listed below. Whenever you use one of these words, you need to know how you're using it: what idea are you trying to get across? Do you mean the word as a noun, a verb, an adjective, a preposition? If you do not know, use your dictionary.

Use your dictionary to determine each word's definition and part of speech. Then circle the correct word.

Example: Before we (accept or except) the offer, we should first consult a lawyer.

According to the dictionary, *accept* is a verb meaning *to receive* and *except* is a preposition meaning *to the exclusion of*. Since *receive* makes sense in the parenthesis while *the exclusion of* does not, *accept* is the correct choice.

Correct: Before we accept the offer, we should first consult a lawyer.

---

1.   Her father tried to give her sound (advice or advise), but she refused to listen to him.

2.   Whatever the counselors (advice or advise), you should listen to them.

3.   Doctors continue to research the (affect or effect) alcohol has on the nervous system.

4.   I do not see how this will (affect or effect) me.

5.   We were (lead or led) to our seats just moments before the house lights went down.

6.   She will (lead or led) us in battle.

7.   He is still trying to estimate the effects of his (loss or lost) on both his personal and business life.

8. I looked everywhere, but the negatives were (loss or lost).

9. Jose thought the team was going to (lose or loose) the game.

10. Although tight clothes are in style, I like to wear things that are (lose or loose).

11. I think I (know or no) the poem well enough to recite it.

12. He has (know or no) understanding of the situation.

13. Because his grades were dropping, Ben was very (quite, quiet, or quit) in class.

14. Mary seemed (quite, quiet, or quit) upset after she hung up the phone.

15. We have lived in our apartment (since or sense) December.

16. His argument makes no (since or sense) unless you have read the book.

17. Mike is quite a bit taller (then or than) his brother.

18. I went to the supermarket, but (then or than) I went out to eat anyway.

19. The professor asked his students to (sight, site or cite) the references they used in their papers.

20. The (sight, site or cite) for the new library will be announced next week.

14. Capitalization Rules

1.   Every sentence must begin with a capital letter.

2.   Capitalize names of persons, titles or abbreviated titles and sacred names.

Capitalize	Do Not Capitalize
John Smith, Ph.D.	man
Dr. Bernadette Williams	doctor
Saint Augustine	saint
President Reagan or the President	president
Mother (when used as a name)	my mother
Grandfather (when used as a name)	the grandfather
God	
the Bible	

3.   Names of specific places and locations (buildings, streets) are capitalized.

Capitalize	Do Not Capitalize
Lowell High School	high school
the Department of Humanities	department
Terrace Drive	drive
16th Street	street
Kansas	state
Empire State Building	building
San Francisco State University	university
Paris, France	city, country

4.   Languages and nationalities are capitalized.

Chinese
Tagalog
Spanish
French
Russian
English
Filipino

5.   Course titles are capitalized, but not the names of specific fields unless they are also the names of languages.

First Year Composition	composition
Psychology 200	psychology
Organic Chemistry II	chemistry
English 50	English

6. Religions:

   Catholic
   Jewish
   Protestant
   Buddhist
   Moslem

7. Specific groups, organizations, institutions, businesses:

   U.S. Army
   The Green Thumb Garden Club
   Supreme Court
   Republican Party
   Prentice©Hall, Inc.
   Moslems

8. Capitalize months, days, holidays, but not seasons.

Capitalize	Do Not Capitalize
October	fall
Friday	summer
Martin Luther King's Birthday	winter

9. Capitalize the first letter of words in titles of books, magazines, plays, stories, movies, etc. except words like *a, an, the, and, of, in* unless they are the first words of the title.

Esquire	*Cats*
For Whom the Bell Toll	*The Color Purple*

10. Capitalize the names of events or periods in history.

    the Renaissance
    World War II
    Watergate

11. Capitalize *north, south, east, west* only when they refer to a specific geographical location.

    Birds fly north in the spring.
    Are we driving east or west?
    Scott is from the Midwest while Vicky is from the Deep South.

Exercise 1

In the following sentences, capitalize the letters that should be capitalized.

---

1. many authors from the deep south have contributed greatly to american literature.

2. my roommate, whose mother never taught her about the value of money, ran up a big bill with pacific telephone.

3. during the month of december, when winter weather is at its worst, sales of sweaters and gloves increase dramatically in department stores all over the north and in the east.

4. my best friend, rosa, speaks both spanish and portuguese and eats potato chips as though they were going out of style.

5. every state in the country has a governor, and california's former governor, chief justice earl warren, also held other positions in california government.

6. there is a street near san francisco state university called sloat boulevard, which is named for commodore sloat.

7. if you travel west on sloat boulevard for a long enough time then you will eventually find yourself in the pacific ocean.

8. during the civil war, president lincoln experienced deep personal sorrow at seeing the north and the south locked in such a bitter political struggle.

9. last year my mother ran the boston marathon, but she wasn't able to finish the first mile.

10. this year, she trained carefully and finished the bay to breakers in excellent time.

Exercise 2

In the following sentences, capitalize letters that should be capitalized and draw a line through the letters that should be lower case.

---

1. after speaking with professor callen, i decided to enroll in principles of organizational management and some other courses in business administration.

2. i met my new boyfriend at the warfield theatre, which is located on market street near mcdonald's and across the street from walgreen's.

3. a good essay is a piece of writing which must be carefully written, says any Good english teacher, but any good, hardworking student can learn how to write well with Time and practice.

4. swallows are birds that fly north, south, East, or west to a City in California called capistrano, but those coming from the eastern part of thc country have the prcttiest trip.

5. members of the feminist movement want to see the equal rights amendment made part of the constitution, while members of the moral majority want to see Abortion made illegal.

6. while I was talking to doctor tarragon about my stomach pains, his nurse came in with some spicy news about his partner, doctor cilantro.

7. when i got the Flu, doctor tarragon told me to take a few tylenol capsules every few hours, but i refused because of the stories i had read in the san francisco chronicle.

8. my Brother-in-law was raised as a catholic, but after attending some of his friends' jewish weddings, he has developed a strong interest in learning about other religions besides his own.

Exercise 3

Proofread the following paragraph, correcting the capitalization.   Insert capitals where they belong and draw a line through capitals that should be small letters.

For christmas my Mother gave me the book, <u>The complete book of Running</u>, by James F. Fixx. Mr. Fixx is from the east and is a graduate of Oberlin college. He started running several years ago on a beautiful Spring morning and since then, he has lost 61 pounds. He competed in six Boston marathons, and he won the Connecticut 10,000 meter Championship in his age category. Running is not the only thing James Fixx is good at; he also is a Writer and former Editor of such Magazines as <u>Life</u>, <u>McCall's</u>, and <u>horizon</u>. He conferred with a number of Doctors in writing his book, as well as the New York academy of sciences and the national institute of mental health. Now that I've read and enjoyed the book, I would like to get dad to read it. Theodore G. Klumpp, m.d., claims that people tend to overprotect them- selves and that older people should exercise more, and he hopes to establish a Nationwide Exercise Program for the elderly. But I know what my Dad would say! He'd tell me he gets plenty of exercise shoveling snow in Kansas and stays healthy with a shot of russian vodka before he goes to bed each night. Besides, dad thinks most of my ideas are Left-wing and he'd probably think jogging is a plot to overthrow the republican party.